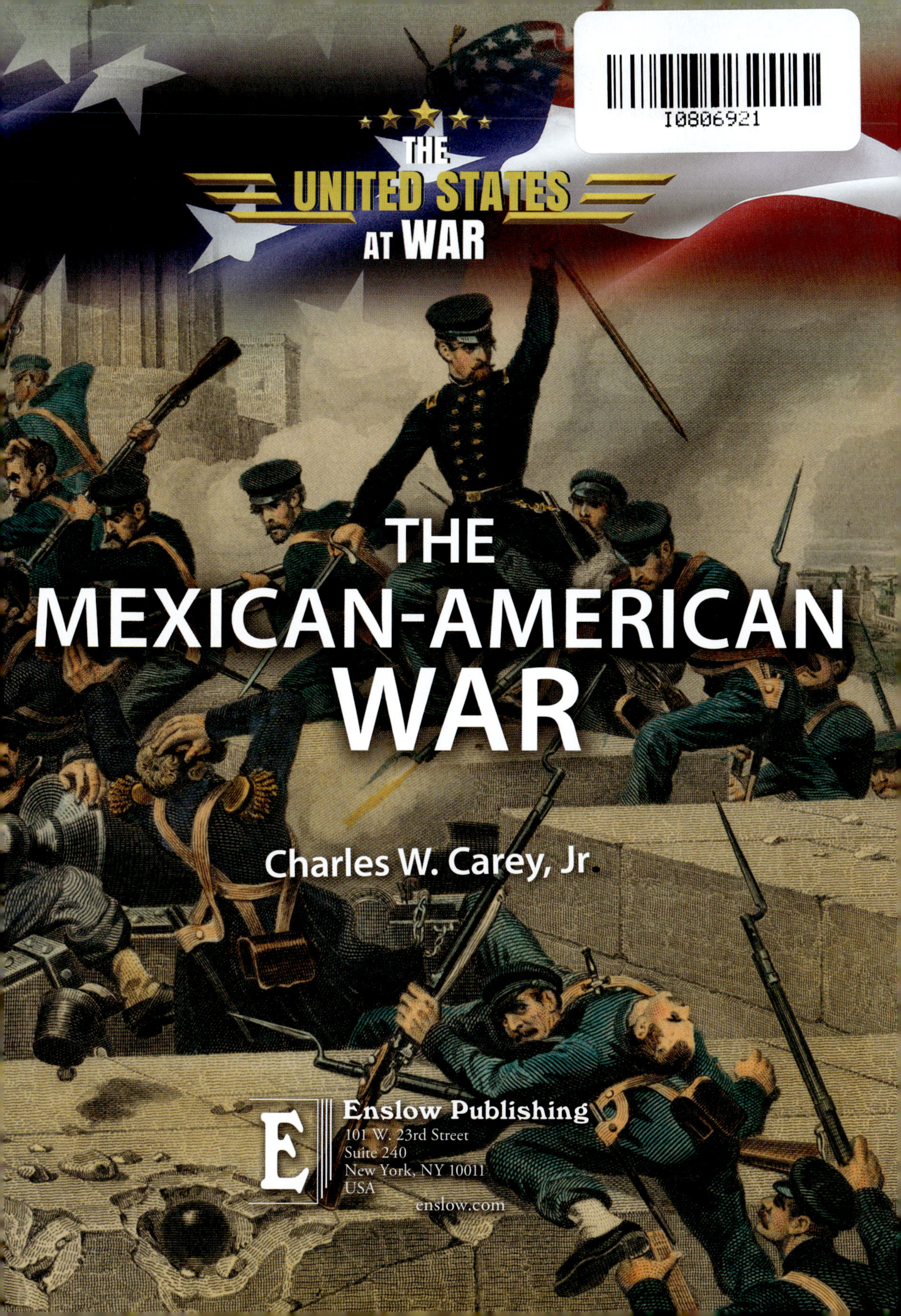

THE UNITED STATES AT WAR

THE MEXICAN-AMERICAN WAR

Charles W. Carey, Jr.

Enslow Publishing
101 W. 23rd Street
Suite 240
New York, NY 10011
USA
enslow.com

Published in 2017 by Enslow Publishing, LLC.
101 W. 23rd Street, Suite 240, New York, NY 10011

Library of Congress Cataloging-in-Publication Data
Names: Carey, Charles W., author.
Title: The Mexican-American War / Charles W. Carey, Jr.
Description: New York, NY : Enslow Publishing, 2017. | Series: The United States at war | Includes bibliographical references and index.
Identifiers: LCCN 2016004688 | ISBN 9780766076624 (library bound)
Subjects: LCSH: Mexican War, 1846-1848.
Classification: LCC E404 .C259 2016 | DDC 973.6/2—dc23
LC record available at http://lccn.loc.gov/2016004688

Printed in the United States of America

To Our Readers: We have done our best to make sure all websites in this book were active and appropriate when we went to press. However, the author and the publisher have no control over and assume no liability for the material available on those websites or on any websites they may link to. Any comments or suggestions can be sent by e-mail to customerservice@enslow.com.

Portions of this book originally appeared in the book *The Mexican War: "Mr. Polk's War."*

Photo Credits: Cover, p. 1 Memory Stockphoto/Shutterstock.com (insignia), Sergey Kamshylin/Shutterstock.com (US flag); Print Collector/Hulton Archive/Getty Images; pp. 4–5; p. 6, 12, 24, 49, 112 Everett Historical/Shutterstock.com; pp. 9, 100, 108 Buyenlarge/Archive Photos/Getty Images; p. 10 Felix Lipov/Shutterstock.com; p. 11 Sanpatricioshang.jpg/Wikimedia commons; p. 15 UnitedStatesExpansion.png/Wikimedia Commons; p. 16 MPI/Archive Photos/Getty Images; p. 20 Interim Archives/Archive Photos/Getty Images; p. 21 Georgios Kollidas/iStock/Thinkstock; pp. 23, 82 © Northwind Archives/AP Images; p. 26 The New York Historical Society/Archive Photos/Getty Images; pp. 31, 68 DEA/G. DAGLI ORTI/De Agostini/Getty Images; pp. 40, 44 DEA PICTURE LIBRARY/De Agostini Picture Library/Getty Images; p. 42 Kean Collection/Archive Photos/Getty Images; pp. 48, 80 Library of Congress, Prints and Photographs Division; p. 50 © Northwind Picture Archives; p. 53 Stephen W. Kearny.jpg/Wikimedia Commons; p. 58 Robert F. StocktonWiki.jpg/Wikimedia Commons; p. 59 ppart/iStock/Thinkstock; p. 60 Ullstein Bild/Getty Images; p. 62 Encyclopedia Britannica/UIG/Getty Images; p. 67 © AP Images; p.70 © Guillermo Lopez Barrera/Alamy Stock Photo; p. 76 Wendy Connett/robertharding/Getty Images; p. 78 Universal Images Group/Getty Images; p. 84 Treaty of Guadalupe Hidalgo.jpg/Wikimedia Commons; p. 86 Felix Lipov/Shutterstock.com; p. 91 Miguel Antonio Otero (18291882).Jpg/Wikimedia Commons; p. 97 Photo Researchers/Science Source/Getty Images; p.110 Archive Photos/Getty Images.

CONTENTS

FOREWORD

"IT SEEMS MOST CREDIBLE THAT OUR LORD GOD HAS PURPOSELY ALLOWED THESE LANDS [MEXICO] TO BE DISCOVERED ... SO THAT YOUR MAJESTIES MAY BE FRUITFUL AND DESERVING IN HIS SIGHT BY CAUSING THESE BARBARIC TRIBES TO BE ENLIGHTENED ..."

—Hernando Cortéz

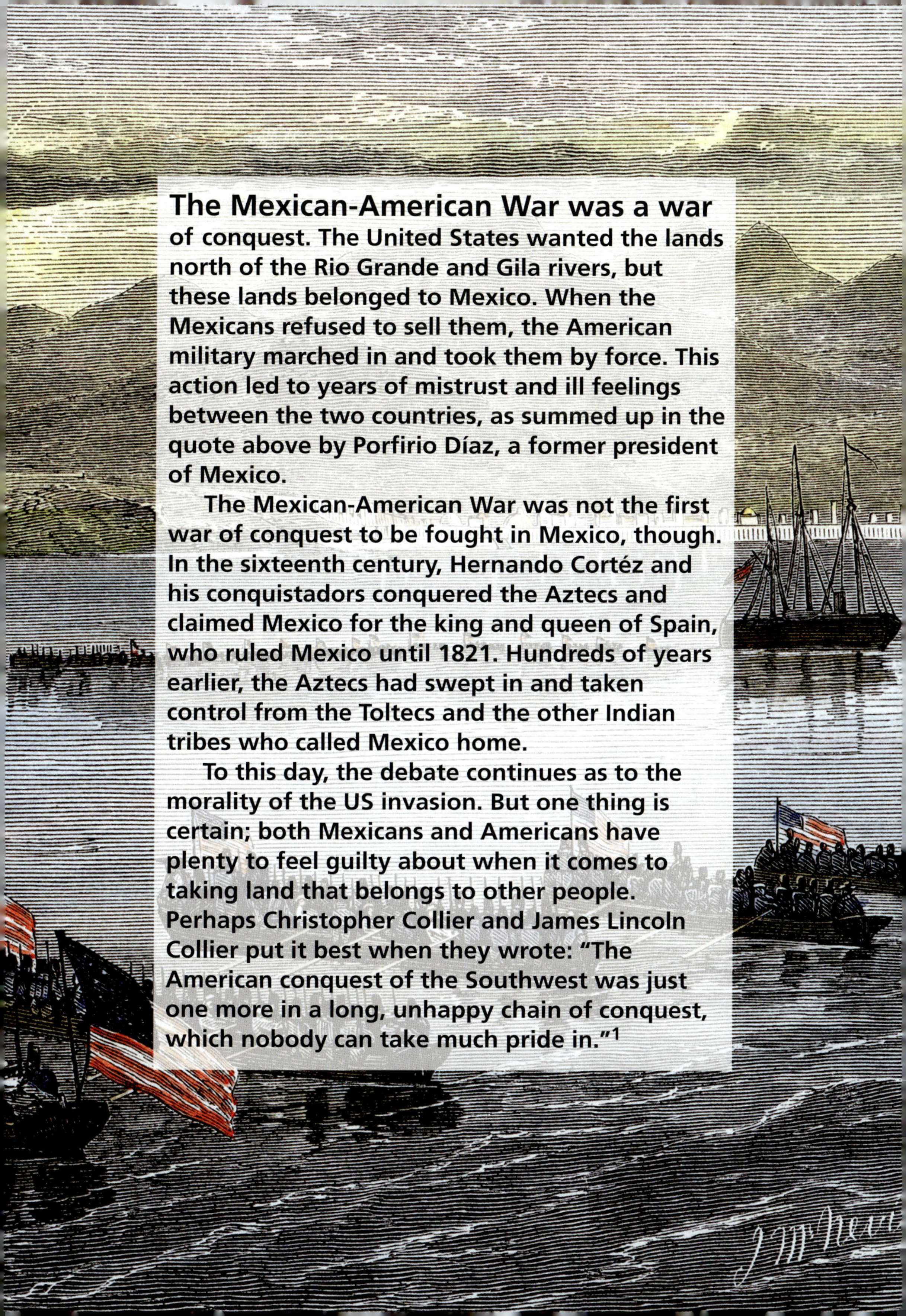

The Mexican-American War was a war of conquest. The United States wanted the lands north of the Rio Grande and Gila rivers, but these lands belonged to Mexico. When the Mexicans refused to sell them, the American military marched in and took them by force. This action led to years of mistrust and ill feelings between the two countries, as summed up in the quote above by Porfirio Díaz, a former president of Mexico.

The Mexican-American War was not the first war of conquest to be fought in Mexico, though. In the sixteenth century, Hernando Cortéz and his conquistadors conquered the Aztecs and claimed Mexico for the king and queen of Spain, who ruled Mexico until 1821. Hundreds of years earlier, the Aztecs had swept in and taken control from the Toltecs and the other Indian tribes who called Mexico home.

To this day, the debate continues as to the morality of the US invasion. But one thing is certain; both Mexicans and Americans have plenty to feel guilty about when it comes to taking land that belongs to other people. Perhaps Christopher Collier and James Lincoln Collier put it best when they wrote: "The American conquest of the Southwest was just one more in a long, unhappy chain of conquest, which nobody can take much pride in."[1]

1

HEROES AND HANGINGS

"POOR MEXICO, SO FAR FROM GOD AND SO CLOSE TO THE UNITED STATES."

—Porfirio Díaz

George E. Pickett was one of the Civil War's most famous generals. He served under General Robert E. Lee in the Army of Northern Virginia at the Battle of Gettysburg. During that battle, Pickett's Division led the way in what is now known as Pickett's Charge, a desperate attempt to break through the Union Army defenses. The charge failed. However, Pickett's Charge was not the first time that Pickett led his troops in a daring attack. The first time was during the Mexican-American War at the Battle of Chapultepec, near Mexico City.

The battle takes its name from the Castle of Chapultepec. This tall fortress stood on a steep hill just outside Mexico City, and it guarded the approach to that city. If the Americans wanted to capture the Mexican capital and win the war, they would have to capture the Castle of Chapultepec.

There were only two ways to get into the castle. One was to knock down the front gate, a large, heavy wooden door that was barred from the inside. The other was to scale the high, thick walls on long, shaky scaling ladders.

The battle began with an American artillery barrage (many cannons firing at the same target) against the castle. The Americans hoped the barrage would demoralize the Mexicans so much that they would surrender. The castle's defenders, however, were too determined. They would not give up without a fight. When the barrage ended, the American infantry (foot soldiers) charged across open ground while the castle's guns fired on them. Those who survived the gunfire from the castle either attacked the front gate or put up their ladders and began climbing.

An American Hero

Pickett, who was a lieutenant at the time, commanded Company A, Eighth Infantry Regiment, and his men were ordered to scale the walls. Luckily for the Americans, the castle was much smaller than it looked. In fact, it was only big enough to hold 250 men inside its walls. Although the defenders fought bravely, there weren't enough of them to keep the Americans from streaming over the walls.

Company A followed another company up the ladders. That other company's flag bearer got shot just after making it over the wall. He handed the flag to his company commander. When that man got shot as well, he handed the flag to Lieutenant Pickett. While the bullets whizzed around him, Pickett carried the flag to the top of the castle. Once he got there, he shot a defender, hauled down the Mexican flag, and in its place raised the Eighth Infantry's regimental flag.

The sight of that flag, and the American flag that joined it moments later, gave the Americans the extra energy they needed to win the battle. At the same time, the sight of their own flag being replaced by the American flags caused many Mexicans to surrender.[1]

Pickett had just recently graduated from West Point when he was called to fight in the Mexican-American War.

Los Niños Héroes

But not all of the castle's defenders surrendered. Many of them were cadets of the Colegio Militar, the Mexican military academy, which was housed in the castle. The cadets were a little younger than the rest of the castle's defenders, mostly in their mid- to late teens. Nicholas Bravo, the Mexican Army general who had taken command of the castle with about two hundred troops, ordered the cadets to leave before the fighting began, but 46 remained to fight. They knew that if the castle could hold out, then maybe the Americans would lose so many men that the brave Mexican Army could finally run them out of Mexico. And after all, they were training to be soldiers. What better training could there be than to fight in a real battle?

According to legend, the cadets were among the last group of Mexican soldiers in the castle to stop fighting. During the battle, six cadets were killed—Fernando Montez de Oca, Juan de la Barrera, Francisco Márquez, Agustin Melgar, Juan Scutia, and Vicente Suárez Ferrer. Another three were wounded and thirty-seven were taken prisoner. The brave cadets became known as *Los Niños Héroes*, or the Heroic Children. They would long be remembered for their heroism in support of their nation.[2]

Hanged for Desertion

One of the units in the Mexican Army was composed mostly of soldiers who were not Mexican. This unit was known as the San Patricio Battalion. Most of its members were Irish Catholic immigrants who had joined the US Army even though they were not US citizens. When their officers did not treat them well, they deserted and joined the Mexican Army. The battalion's name is Spanish for Saint Patrick, the

This monument in Mexico City remembers the courage of the Niños Héroes during the Battle of Chapultepec.

Samuel Chamberlain painted the hanging of the San Patricios after the Battle of Chapultepec in the 1840s.

patron saint of Ireland.

The San Patricios were some of the bravest soldiers in the Mexican Army. They had fought courageously just a few days before at the Convent of San Mateo, during the Battle of Churubusco on the outskirts of Mexico City. Despite their bravery, many of the San Patricios were captured at Churubusco and sentenced to death for being traitors. Thirty San Patricios were scheduled to be hanged as soon as the Castle of Chapultepec fell to the Americans.

While the battle was taking place, the thirty deserters were forced to stand in wagons with hangman's nooses around their necks. All of them knew that as soon as the American flag appeared in victory above the walls of the castle, they would be hanged. Instead of begging for their lives, the Irishmen hooted and jeered at their guards. But eventually their time on earth came to an end. As soon as Lieutenant Pickett raised his flag over the Castle of Chapultepec, thirty horses were whipped, thirty wagons jerked forward, and the thirty San Patricios were left to twist in the wind.[3]

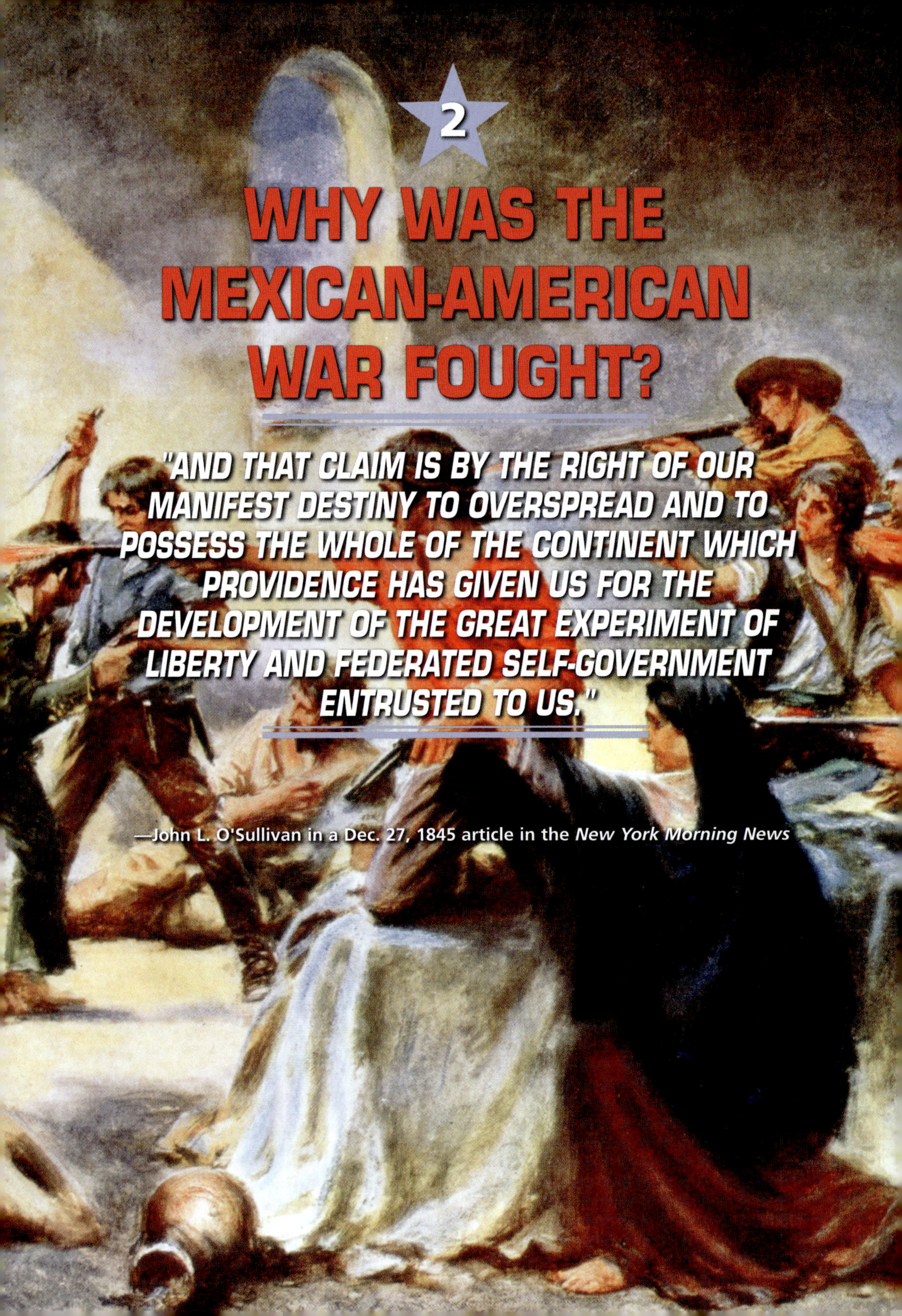

2

WHY WAS THE MEXICAN-AMERICAN WAR FOUGHT?

"AND THAT CLAIM IS BY THE RIGHT OF OUR MANIFEST DESTINY TO OVERSPREAD AND TO POSSESS THE WHOLE OF THE CONTINENT WHICH PROVIDENCE HAS GIVEN US FOR THE DEVELOPMENT OF THE GREAT EXPERIMENT OF LIBERTY AND FEDERATED SELF-GOVERNMENT ENTRUSTED TO US."

—John L. O'Sullivan in a Dec. 27, 1845 article in the *New York Morning News*

In the American Revolution and the War of 1812, the United States fought to obtain and then preserve American independence. But in the Mexican-American War, American troops fought to gain new territory for the United States. Many Americans thought that going to war with Mexico was a good idea. Many others, however, opposed the war because they thought it was an unjustified act of aggression. Mexicans agreed with this latter group, and to this day most Mexicans think of the Mexican-American War as a "Yankee invasion."[1]

What led the United States to go to war against Mexico? There were two reasons for the outbreak of the Mexican-American War, one long term and the other short term. The long-term reason was the idea of Manifest Destiny. This belief, extremely popular among nineteenth-century Americans, claimed that the United States had been chosen by God to rule the North American continent between the Atlantic and Pacific oceans and between the Great Lakes and the Rio Grande. The short-term reason was the United States' recent annexation of the independent Republic of Texas, which was still claimed by Mexico. Manifest Destiny led Americans into a war with Mexico, while the desire to regain Texas led the Mexicans into a war with the United States.

Jefferson Buys Louisiana

In the early days of the Republic, most Americans made their living by farming. This meant that the United States had to be big enough so that its people could have enough land to farm. For a while, Americans seemed content controlling the land east of the Mississippi River and between Canada and Florida. In 1800, most Americans still lived east of the Appalachian Mountains. Although Kentucky was largely settled, much of the land west of the Appalachians was forest inhabited by Native Americans. It seemed as if the United States owned enough land to take care of future population growth for a long time to come.

American attitudes about expansion began to change in 1803 when the United States bought the Louisiana Territory from France. At first, President

The Louisiana Purchase (in white), which nearly doubled the territory of the United States, led Americans to dream of controlling all the land in North America from coast to coast.

Thomas Jefferson wanted to buy just the city of New Orleans because it controlled the mouth of the Mississippi River. If the United States owned New Orleans, then farmers west of the Appalachians could ship their goods to the eastern states by boat down the Ohio and Mississippi rivers to New Orleans, and from there up the east coast by ship. Although longer, this water route was faster and cheaper than hauling farm products by wagon across the Appalachians. When the French offered to include all of their Louisiana lands between the Mississippi River and the Rocky Mountains as part of the New Orleans sale, Jefferson jumped at the chance, buying Louisiana for $15 million. As a result of the Louisiana Purchase, the United States extended its borders two thirds of the way from the Atlantic Ocean to the Pacific Ocean.[2]

Pushing the Boundaries

From 1803 to 1819, they claimed that Texas, the northeast corner of New Spain (modern-day Mexico), was part of the Louisiana Purchase. The reason for this claim was that the boundaries of the Louisiana

Territory were not well defined. The Americans also wanted to take over Florida, another Spanish possession, because the Seminole Indians who lived there often raided Americans living in Georgia. In 1819, the United States Army invaded Florida to put an end to these raids. The Spanish knew they could not defend Florida against any more US attacks so they offered to give Florida to the United States if the United States would give up its claim to Texas. This offer was accepted.

For years, the United States had tried to gain control of Oregon Country (modern-day Oregon, Washington, and Idaho), another area of incredibly rich farmland. However, in 1818 it agreed to share Oregon Country with the British for twenty years after realizing that the British would not give up their claim to the territory without a fight—something the United States wanted to avoid at this time.[3]

Here, American troops hunt down Native Americans in Florida during the Second Seminole War.

Manifest Destiny

After 1840, immigration to the United States increased dramatically. As more people arrived, the eastern states became more crowded, which encouraged more Americans to move to the lands west of the Mississippi River. In 1845, John L. O'Sullivan, the editor of *United States Magazine and Democratic Review*, spurred them to action by putting their feelings into powerful words. O'Sullivan wrote that it was America's "manifest destiny to overspread the continent allotted by Providence." He meant that he believed it was God's will that Americans should govern all of North America, including Canada and Mexico. A number of American politicians and newspaper editors echoed O'Sullivan's call to action. The phrase *Manifest Destiny* quickly became part of the American political language.[4]

Manifest Destiny seemed to go hand in hand with the Monroe Doctrine. In December 1823, President James Monroe had proclaimed that the United States would not tolerate any European interference in the new nations of Central and South America that had just gained their independence from Spain (ironically, one of those new nations was Mexico). This meant that the United States saw itself as the power in charge of both North America and South America.

Although most Americans believed in Manifest Destiny, few could agree on exactly which lands the United States was supposed to govern. Nor could they agree on whether those lands should be captured by American troops or bought with American dollars. Some thought that the British should be driven out of Canada, even though that had proven to be impossible before. Others urged that Mexico and Central America should become part of the United States. Some wanted to take over the Caribbean islands and South America, and some even talked about acquiring some of the Pacific islands, like Hawaii and Samoa, and parts of Asia. But just about everyone who believed in Manifest Destiny agreed that it meant annexing Texas, obtaining Oregon from the British, and obtaining California and New Mexico from the Mexicans.[5]

By 1847, the ownership of Oregon Country was settled. Although both the United States and Great Britain had threatened to go to war over Oregon, neither really wanted to, and so they agreed to split Oregon in two. The British kept the northern half (modern-day British Columbia) and the Americans kept the southern half, which included modern-day Oregon, Washington, Idaho, and parts of Montana and Wyoming.[6]

Obtaining California and New Mexico proved to be a harder task than obtaining Oregon. So did obtaining Texas.

Texas Becomes Independent

After Mexico obtained its independence from Spain in 1821, the United States tried to buy Texas from the Mexicans. Instead of selling, the Mexicans invited private American citizens to settle in Texas. The Mexican government was concerned that Texas was not heavily populated enough to keep the United States from taking it by force. Only about 3,500 Mexicans and an unknown number of Native Americans, mostly Apache and Comanche, lived in Texas at the time. The Mexicans believed that, if they could get more settlers to come to Texas, then the economy would improve and tax revenues would increase. They also hoped that Americans settling in Texas could be made into loyal citizens of Mexico, making the United States think twice before they tried to take the territory. So, in 1824, Mexico offered cheap land and low taxes to any American who would settle in Texas. Of course, new settlers had to pledge allegiance to Mexico. They also had to become Roman Catholic (the official religion of Mexico), and they had to promise to give up slavery.

At first, the plan seemed to work. Over the next six years, 7,000 Americans settled in Texas, including Stephen Austin, Sam Houston, and Jim Bowie, who would become famous for their adventures there. Most of them came to plant cotton and other crops, and the Texas economy began to boom.

Unfortunately for Mexico, most of the Americans who settled in Texas remained loyal to the United States, despite whatever pledges they made. And many of these American settlers also insisted on owning slaves, which was illegal in Mexico. The Mexican government was alarmed by these developments, and in 1830 it banned any more Americans from settling in Texas. By now, however, it was too late. Over the next five years, Americans continued to settle in Texas. By 1835, the American population in Texas was almost 40,000, far more than the number of Mexicans living in Texas.[7]

In 1835, the Mexican government tried to tighten its authority over Texas. But the Texans resisted, and in 1836, they declared their independence from Mexico. At first, it seemed that the Mexican government would easily crush the revolt. The president of Mexico, General Antonio López de Santa Anna, personally led an army of 6,000 men into Texas. At the Battle of the Alamo, an old Spanish mission in San Antonio, the Mexicans completely wiped out the Alamo's 183 defenders, although the badly outnumbered Americans put up a spirited fight that lasted for days. Among those killed were the famous frontiersmen Davy Crockett and Jim Bowie. Then, at the Battle of Goliad, the Mexicans massacred 350 Texans rather than take them prisoner. Despite these defeats, the American forces under Sam Houston vowed to keep fighting. At the Battle of San Jacinto, the Texans were able to turn the tables on the Mexicans. According to legend, Sam Houston's army of 800 men caught the Mexicans taking a siesta (a midday nap) and slaughtered most of them before they were awake and ready to fight. They even managed to capture General Santa Anna, and forced him to sign a treaty granting Texas its independence. Although the Mexican government

Here, Mexican soldiers attack the Texans trying to hold the Alamo. The Texans held out for 13 days before the Mexicans killed all the defenders.

rejected the treaty and still believed Texas belonged to Mexico, it never sent another army into Texas.[8]

Texas Tries to Join the Union

In 1836, Texas, now calling itself the independent Republic of Texas, applied for admission as a state to the United States. For nine years, Congress debated the issue. At first, the Senate was reluctant to admit Texas, partly because it feared a war with Mexico, so the application was rejected. As time went on, however, war with Mexico seemed less likely, considering the fact that the Mexicans had never tried to recapture Texas even though they still claimed it. Many Americans now feared that an independent Texas would acquire New Mexico and California before the United States could do so.

James Polk became president through a campaign supporting Manifest Destiny. When he took office, he set out to win territory for the United States—even if it meant going to war with Mexico to get it.

The annexation of Texas became the most important issue of the election of 1844. Campaigning on a platform that strongly supported Manifest Destiny, Democrat James K. Polk was elected president. Polk and the Democrats favored the annexation of Texas, and in 1845 they were able to persuade Congress to make Texas a state. However, Mexico still claimed Texas, and it protested the annexation by breaking off diplomatic relations with the United States.[9]

In 1845, Polk sent John Slidell to Mexico City to offer the Mexicans $30 million for California and New Mexico. However, the Mexicans were still upset over the annexation of Texas and they refused to even listen to Slidell's offer. Instead, they promised to take back Texas.[10]

Border War

The Mexican-American War began as a border dispute between the United States and Mexico. The Texans claimed that the Rio Grande, a river that flows into the Gulf of Mexico near Matamoros, was the border between Texas and Mexico. The Mexicans disagreed. They claimed that the Nueces River, which flows into the Gulf of Mexico at Corpus Christi, about 200 miles (322 km) to the north of Matamoros, was the border. The area between the two rivers contained much of what the Mexicans considered New Mexico. Neither side pressed its claim until the United States annexed Texas.

After annexing Texas in 1845, the United States insisted that Mexico observe the Rio Grande as the border. In January 1846, Polk ordered General Zachary Taylor to take 4,000 men—at that time half of the entire United States Army—and occupy a position on the Rio Grande near Matamoros, where 3,000 Mexican troops were stationed.

For three months, both sides eyed each other cautiously. Shooting broke out in April when an 11-man American patrol looking for a missing officer was ambushed and wiped out. A few days later,

The darker yellow part of this map shows the land controlled by Mexico in the 1840s, before the Mexican-American War was fought.

another American patrol was ambushed. This time, 63 men were killed, wounded, or captured.

Ever since Mexico had refused to talk to Slidell, and refused to acknowledge that Texas belonged to the United States, President Polk had been looking for a way to secure Texas once and for all. These border incidents gave him just what he needed. On May 11, 1846, Polk asked Congress to declare war against Mexico, claiming that the Mexicans had "shed the blood of our fellow-citizens on our own soil."[11] Not all congressmen were convinced of the truth of Polk's claim. But most congressmen were in favor of war and the chance to win new territory for the United States. The day after Polk's request, both the House and the Senate voted to declare war against Mexico.[12]

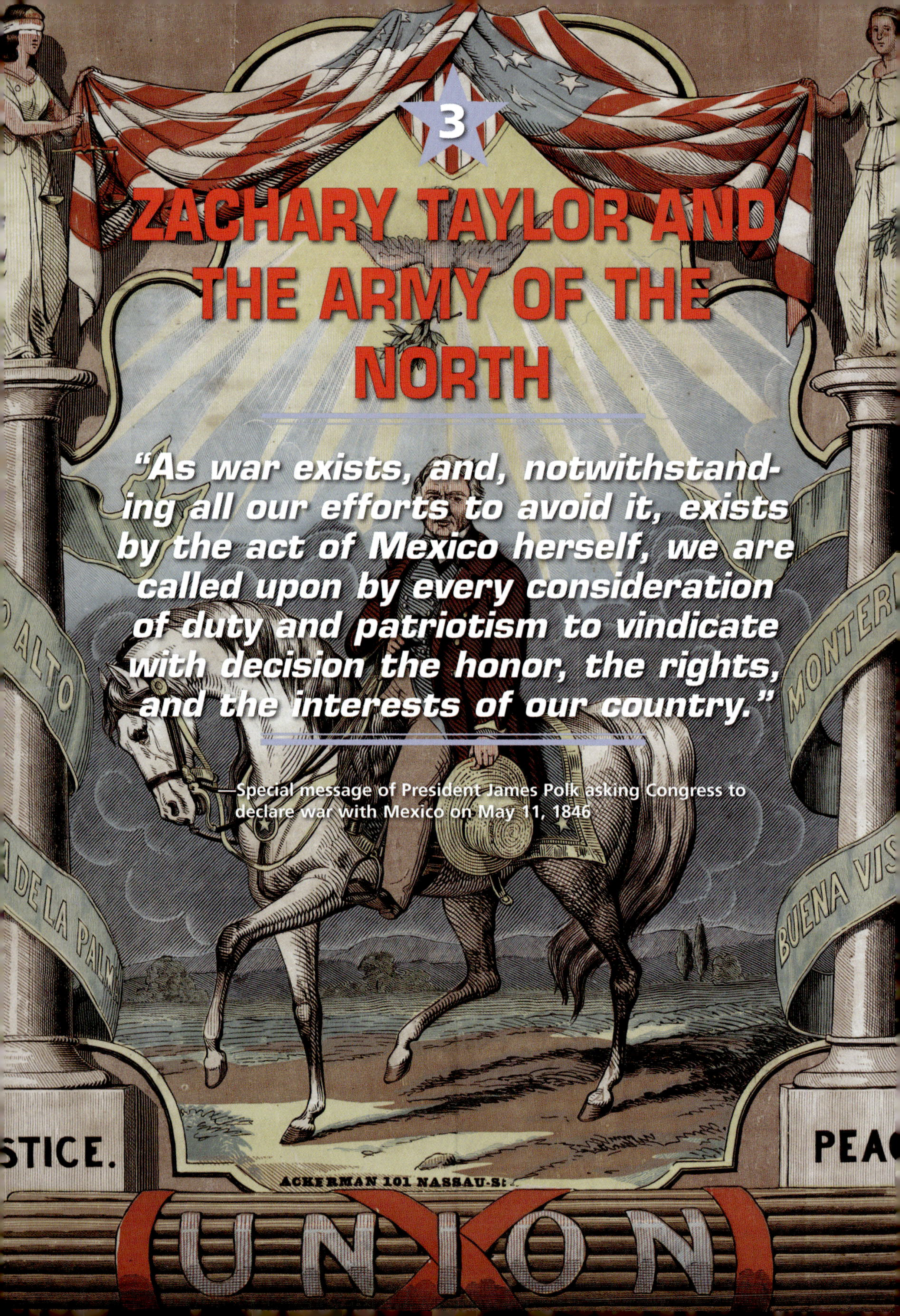

3

ZACHARY TAYLOR AND THE ARMY OF THE NORTH

"As war exists, and, notwithstanding all our efforts to avoid it, exists by the act of Mexico herself, we are called upon by every consideration of duty and patriotism to vindicate with decision the honor, the rights, and the interests of our country."

—Special message of President James Polk asking Congress to declare war with Mexico on May 11, 1846

Zachary Taylor was not the typical American general. He hated to wear his dress uniform and preferred to dress in old, beat-up clothes. Many visitors to his headquarters mistook him for an orderly. One young lieutenant, who obviously did not know what the general looked like, even offered him a dollar to clean his sword! But Taylor's men loved him because he was one of the few officers willing to share in their suffering. If they went hungry or thirsty or slept out in the open, then so did he. Because of all this, Taylor's men affectionately nicknamed him "Old Rough and Ready."[1]

Here, Zachary Taylor is shown before the Battle of Monterrey. His victories during the Mexican-American War won him the US presidency in 1849.

The first order of business for the Army of Occupation, as Taylor's army was called, was to occupy the disputed territory between the Rio Grande and Nueces rivers. After leaving Corpus Christi in late March, Taylor's army marched south without meeting any Mexican resistance. After establishing a supply base at Point Isabel, just north of the Rio Grande on the Gulf of Mexico, Taylor concentrated most of his forces at Fort Texas (later renamed Fort Brown). The fort was just across the river from Matamoros where 3,000 Mexican troops, under the command of General Pedro de Ampudia, were stationed.

Ampudia was greatly feared by his men. He had a reputation for being cruel. In 1844, after ordering the execution of a prisoner named Francisco Sentmanat, Ampudia had Sentmanat's head fried in oil so it would last longer on public display.

From Fort Texas and Point Isabel, the Americans could easily control the disputed area between the two rivers. But in late April, Matamoros was reinforced by an additional 3,000 Mexican troops. The entire command of the Mexican Army of the North (so called because it fought in northern Mexico) was given to General Mariano Arista, one of the Mexican Army's best generals. Unlike Ampudia, Arista had a reputation for treating his troops fairly. Suddenly, Taylor's Army of Occupation found itself outnumbered 6,000 to 4,000 and facing a force commanded by a popular, competent general.[2]

Outnumbered but Not Outclassed

Though they were outnumbered, the Americans had three important advantages. First, all of Taylor's troops were trained professionals. These men had volunteered for military service because they wanted to make the army their career. They had been drilled and disciplined for many months. They were equipped with modern firearms, durable uniforms, and high-quality leather boots. They were fed wholesome food, they had plenty of water to drink, and they were provided with decent medical care. In addition, as citizens who had a right to vote, many felt they had a personal stake in a war that affected their country's future.

Most of the Mexican troops, on the other hand, were Indians and peasants who had little training as soldiers. The Mexican infantry was equipped mostly with hand-me-down muskets bought cheaply from the British Army, and they did not always have enough ammunition or gunpowder. Many soldiers wore civilian clothes. Some wore sandals instead of boots. They often had to scrounge for food and water, and they rarely received medical treatment. In addition, they had no role in Mexican politics, so their willingness to fight for their country was low. In fact, the only reason many of them were serving in the army at all was because they had been forced to become soldiers by the Mexican government.[3]

The Americans' second advantage was that the United States Army artillery corps was one of the world's best. American artillerymen were trained to fire rapidly and accurately. Their biggest guns were twenty-four-pounders (guns that fired a cannonball or shell weighing twenty-four pounds), which were accurate at ranges up to 1 mile (1.6 km). The Americans also had a number of light artillery batteries that used six- and twelve-pounders. These guns were so light that they could be limbered (attached to horses for transport) quickly and hauled within minutes to wherever they were needed on the battlefield. They could then be unlimbered just as rapidly and used to support an attack on a weak enemy position or to defend against a strong enemy attack. These batteries could travel so fast that they seemed to fly across the battlefield, and so they were often called "flying artillery."[4]

They would be up against the Mexican artillery corps—one of the world's worst. Like the infantry, the Mexican artillerymen were not well trained.

Their biggest guns were eighteen-pounders, and their range was much shorter than the American guns. Most importantly, the Mexicans had no flying artillery, so it took them much longer to get their guns in place.

The United States' third advantage was its naval forces. The United States Navy was far superior to the Mexican Navy. American ships were faster, more numerous, and better armed than Mexican ships. In no time, the United States Navy's Home Squadron blockaded the entire Gulf Coast of Mexico. This meant that General Taylor's army could be supplied and reinforced by sea at its base at Point Isabel rather than by long overland supply lines that could be easily attacked. It also meant that the Mexican Army, which was poorly supplied to begin with, could not receive any additional weapons or supplies from overseas.

Throughout the war, the Home Squadron played a small but important role. Merchant ships under the squadron's protection delivered supplies for the American Army quickly and efficiently. In addition to blockading the major Mexican Gulf ports of Matamoros, Tampico, and Veracruz, the squadron also landed marines at a number of smaller harbors to prevent small ships from landing supplies that would aid the Mexicans.

Palo Alto

Arista tried to take advantage of his superior numbers by attacking first. On May 1, he sent the main body of his army across the Rio Grande to the east of Fort Texas while the rest of his men crossed

American volunteers who were now arriving at his camp. These volunteers had enlisted for ninety days and were organized into state regiments that were commanded by civilian officers. For the most part, these volunteer units lacked training and discipline. Worst of all, Taylor lacked the necessary food, drinking water, tents, and medical supplies to supply and maintain them. It took Taylor over two months—out of the three they would be there for—to outfit and organize the volunteers for battle.

During these months, the volunteers got a good taste of the realities of war. They had left home dreaming of becoming war heroes. Now they found themselves hanging around the American camp with nothing to do, not enough to eat or drink, and too little shelter from the hot days and cold nights of northern Mexico. One of the army camps was located next to a swamp, and the soldiers were constantly bothered by mosquitoes and mud. Other camps had it better. There, the men had only to deal with snakes, scorpions, spiders, and lots and lots of ants. Sadly, during these two months 1,500 volunteers—far more than were killed by the Mexicans in battle—died from disease and exposure to the elements without ever seeing action against the enemy. Of those who survived, many either deserted or simply returned home after their ninety-day enlistment expired.[10]

The Armies Move South

After losing most of his army at the Battle of Resaca de la Palma, Arista abandoned Matamoros and retreated to Monterrey, the most important city in northeastern Mexico. Disgusted by Arista's performance, Mexican President Mariano Paredes put General Pedro de Ampudia back in charge. Paredes also saw to it that the Army of the North was reinforced so that, by September, Ampudia had almost 10,000 men.[11]

Meanwhile, Taylor was making plans to chase the Army of the North into Monterrey. He ordered the American Army of Occupation to move up the Rio Grande to Camargo, about 100 miles (161 km) northeast of Monterrey. Once he got there, he realized how difficult it would be to cross the desert between Camargo and Monterrey with all his men and supplies. So he decided to take only 3,000 of 7,700 volunteers as well as the remaining 3,200 regulars, for a total force 6,200. Once again, the Army of Occupation would be outnumbered by the Army of the North.[12]

Monterrey

Taylor's men met little resistance until they reached the northern outskirts of Monterrey on September 19. They quickly realized that taking the city would not be as easy as reaching it had been. The north side of Monterrey was protected by the Citadel, a dark, castle-like fortress that the Americans called the Black Fort. The east side was defended by El Tenería, an old tannery building whose walls had been reinforced, and El Diablo (the Devil's Fort), which was made of stone. The west side was guarded by the Bishop's Palace on the Mountain of Obispado (also known as Independence Hill) and El Soldado (The Soldier) on Federacion Hill. The south side was protected by the Santa Catarina River and the Sierra Madre mountains. In addition, many of the buildings in Monterrey were made of stone, making the entire city one huge fortress.

After studying the situation, Taylor decided his best bet was to attack from the west. The Bishop's Palace sat atop a steep hill covered with chaparral. The Americans might be able to sneak up the hill, under cover of the chaparral, and capture the palace without suffering too many casualties. Then they could place their guns in the palace and fire on the city and the other forts. From the palace they could also control the road to Saltillo, the primary route by which the Army of the North received reinforcements and supplies. Taking command of that road would isolate Monterrey from the rest of Mexico, which might make the Mexicans surrender the city.[13]

With this plan in mind, Taylor split his army into two groups. The smaller group, General William J. Worth's brigade of about 2,000 men, was sent to slip past the Black Fort and attack the Bishop's Palace. The larger group included Taylor's other three brigades. They would attempt to draw away attention from Worth's attack by attacking El Tenería and El Diablo on the east side of town.

Worth's men spent most of September 20, 1846, getting into position to attack the palace. After a skirmish (minor battle) with some Mexican cavalry, they reached the base of the Mountain of Obispado, atop which sat the Bishop's Palace. Worth realized that the palace would be easier to capture if his men first took El Soldado, the fort to the south.

Federacion Hill, on which El Soldado stood, was not as well defended as the Mountain of Obispado, and El Soldado would serve as a good place to mount artillery for the assault against the palace. Also, since it was south of the palace, controlling El Soldado would permit the Americans to attack the palace from three sides.

While about half of Worth's brigade created a diversion by attacking the palace, the other half set off to attack El Soldado. By late afternoon, the Americans had reached the top of the hill and captured a nine-pounder from the Mexicans. When this gun was turned on the fort, El Soldado's 200 defenders panicked and fled. On their first day of fighting, Worth's men had captured El Soldado and Federacion Hill while suffering minimal casualties.[14]

As part of his diversion in support of Worth, Taylor ordered an artillery barrage against the Black Fort. He also sent a brigade of about 1,200 men to attack El Tenería, which was defended by 200 Mexicans. This attack quickly bogged down when the Americans encountered deadly fire from El Tenería as well as from El Diablo, the Black Fort, and the rooftops of many houses. But rather than fall back after putting on a show as Taylor had intended, the brigade pressed forward with its attack. By day's end, it had captured El Tenería, but it had to be reinforced with more men, and it suffered heavy casualties in the process.[15]

Taylor sent another brigade to force its way into the north end of town. Caught in the crossfire between the guns of the Black Fort and the musket fire from rooftops, these men also suffered heavy casualties while being repulsed several times. Altogether, the attacks on the Black Fort and El Tenería cost the Americans almost 400 killed and wounded on the first day of battle.[16]

September 22 was rainy and windy. A detachment of Worth's brigade took advantage of the bad weather and the predawn darkness to creep up through the thick chaparral on the Mountain of Obispado's west slope. They were not seen until they reached the top, and they quickly chased away the Mexican defenders.

Some American artillerymen then dragged a twelve-pounder up the mountain and opened fire on the Bishop's Palace, while about 1,000 infantrymen scrambled up the mountain and stormed the palace. Meanwhile, other artillerymen opened fire on the palace from El Soldado. In desperation, the palace's 200 Mexican defenders charged the American infantry position, but most were either cut down or forced to flee. By late afternoon, Worth's men, who had suffered only thirty-two casualties in two days, were finally in complete control of the palace. They were now in an excellent position to swoop down on Monterrey from the west.

Although his men were still eager to fight, Ampudia realized that the success of Worth's attack had cut off his army from reinforcements and supplies. He also feared that American artillery posted at the palace and El Soldado would slowly pound his troops in the city to pieces. In a fit of panic he ordered his men to abandon their positions and to join him in downtown Monterrey. Ampudia then began planning for a breakout attack (when a surrounded army tries to fight its way through enemy lines).[17]

On September 23, Taylor's three other brigades renewed their attacks on Monterrey's north and east defenses. Although they still drew fire from the Mexicans in the Black Fort, they were greatly relieved to find that the city's rooftop defenders had pulled back and were no longer fighting as ferociously as they had two days earlier. Several detachments were able to penetrate the Mexican defenses to within a block of the city's central plaza. Satisfied that the city could now be taken, General Taylor sent some troops to occupy El Diablo. Then he pulled the rest of the three brigades back from their probing attacks and prepared to assault the city the next day.

While the rest of the army was probing Monterrey's defenses, Worth's brigade heard the gunfire from the fighting in the city below and charged down the Mountain of Obispado into the west end of Monterrey. The infantry fought from house to house, while the artillerymen began shelling the central plaza.

By now, Ampudia had had enough. Cut off from reinforcements and supplies and surrounded on three sides by enemy artillery, on September 24, he sent one of his officers to ask Taylor what his terms of surrender would be. After much negotiating, the two sides agreed that the Army of the North would be allowed to leave Monterrey in peace. However, the army could take with it no weapons other than six artillery guns and the officers' swords and pistols.

There were many casualties during the Battle of Monterrey.

In addition, the two sides agreed to an eight-week truce so that their governments could have the opportunity to work out a permanent peace settlement. By the end of September, the Mexicans had departed. Monterrey was in the hands of the United States Army.[18]

What to Do Next?

The official American reaction to Taylor's victory at Monterrey was mixed. General Winfield Scott, the United States Army's general in chief, called the battle "three glorious days." President James K. Polk, on the other hand, was furious that Taylor had let Ampudia's army escape. He was also angry that Taylor had signed a truce.[19]

The situation in northern Mexico caused Polk and Scott to rethink their basic strategy for winning the war, which was to march due south from Texas to Mexico City. Despite their victory, Taylor's men were almost completely exhausted. The farther they got from the Rio Grande, the harder it was to supply and reinforce them. There were still almost 1,000 miles (1,609 km) of mountainous terrain between them and Mexico City. And the Mexican Army of the North, although disarmed for the moment, could easily round up enough weapons to make it a powerful fighting force once again, especially if a skillful general could be found to lead it.

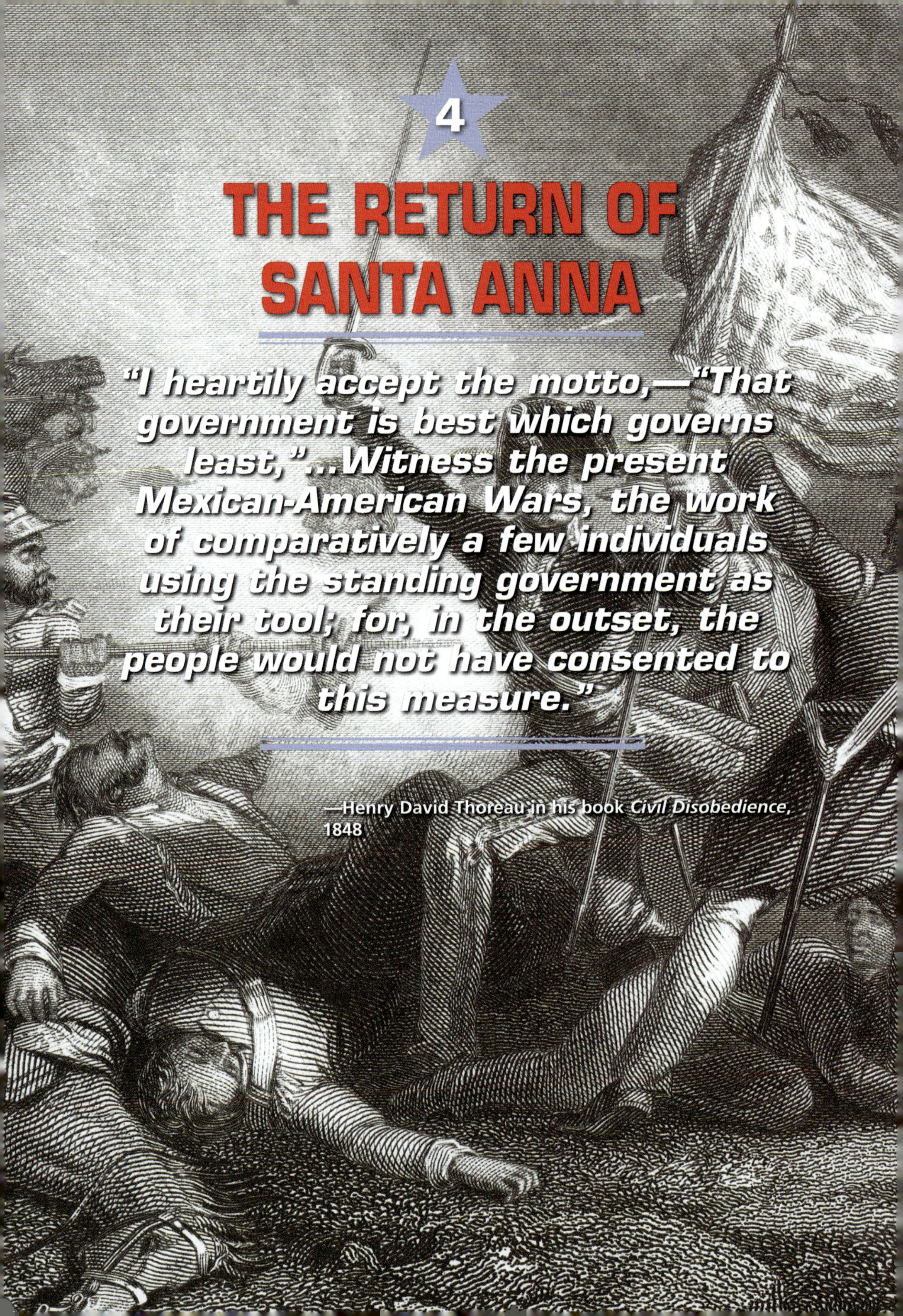

4

THE RETURN OF SANTA ANNA

"I heartily accept the motto,—"That government is best which governs least,"...Witness the present Mexican-American Wars, the work of comparatively a few individuals using the standing government as their tool; for, in the outset, the people would not have consented to this measure."

—Henry David Thoreau in his book *Civil Disobedience*, 1848

The search for that general did not take very long at all. In the end, there was only one man who could lead Mexico to victory in its hour of greatest need. That man was Antonio López de Santa Anna, one of the most remarkable figures in Mexican history.

Santa Anna had been a soldier almost all of his life. He joined the army at the age of sixteen. He fought against the Spanish in 1821 when Mexico won its independence, and again in 1829 when the Spanish tried unsuccessfully to retake Mexico.

In 1836, while serving as the President of Mexico, he led the Mexican Army to victory against the Texans at the Alamo and Goliad, only to lose to them at San Jacinto. He was captured at San Jacinto, shipped off to Washington, DC, as a prisoner of war, and eventually returned to Mexico.

In 1838, the French Army captured Veracruz, on the Gulf of Mexico, in an effort to get the Mexican government to pay its debts to France. Santa Anna led the troops that forced the French to leave Veracruz, and in the fighting, one of his legs was blown off. Hailed as a hero, he became president of Mexico for a second time in 1841. Three years later, he was driven out by his political enemies in 1844 and forced to leave the country. In 1846, he managed to get the Americans to sneak him back into Mexico after the war broke out by promising that he would work for a peace treaty favorable to the United States. Upon his return to Mexico, he was hailed as a hero once again.

Santa Anna had a 40-year career as a leader in Mexico. He served as the Mexican president eleven times over twenty-two years.

Most Mexicans believed that Santa Anna

was the only general they had who could drive the Americans out of Mexico. In 1846, he was made president of Mexico for a third time. Once again, he took control of the Mexican military—this time, to get rid of Zachary Taylor's Army of Occupation.

Santa Anna was filled with energy, imagination, and optimism. Where others saw the end, he saw only a new beginning. His charismatic personality and impressive skills as a public speaker won him the affection and support of the Mexican upper class. His fondness for drinking and gambling won him the affection and support of the Mexican lower class, including the military men who served under him. His hero was Napoleon Bonaparte, the legendary French general who almost conquered all of Europe. Santa Anna was pleased and proud to be known in Mexico as "the Napoleon of the West."[1]

On September 28, 1846, Santa Anna headed north from Mexico City with a small force. By October 8, he had reached San Luis Potosi, about 300 miles (483 km) south of Monterrey. Here, he met up with the retreating Army of the North. He immediately made himself the army's new commander. Then he spent the next few months rebuilding the Army of the North into an effective fighting force.

Buena Vista

While Santa Anna was transforming the Army of the North, Zachary Taylor was exploring the terrain south of Monterrey to see if he could march through it to Mexico City. He sent one brigade to Saltillo, about 50 miles (80 km) southwest of Monterrey, to check out the area. Then he sent two other brigades marching to the east to help the United States Navy's Home Squadron capture Tampico for use as a naval base. Taking their place was General John E. Wool's brigade of 1,300 regular soldiers and volunteers. These changes left Taylor with an army of 4,800 men, or about 1,400 fewer than he had when he attacked Monterrey.

Meanwhile, Santa Anna had built up his army to more than 15,000 men. On January 28, he began marching it north to attack Taylor. At the same time, Taylor's army was slowly advancing toward Agua Nueva, about 20 miles (32 km) south of Saltillo. The two armies would battle it out at Buena Vista.

Advance units of the two armies first made contact on February 20 at Agua Nueva, which sat in the middle of a broad valley. It was a bad place for an outnumbered army to defend. So Taylor pulled his men back to La Angostura, a narrow pass in the mountains just south of the village of Hacienda de Buena Vista, about 6 miles (10 km) south of Saltillo.

Taylor posted one brigade to defend the two main routes through the mountains to Buena Vista. The 1st Illinois and 3rd Indiana volunteer regiments guarded the main road from San Luis Potosi to Saltillo, while the 2nd Indiana, 2nd Illinois, and 2nd Kentucky volunteer regiments guarded a pass to the east of the road. Both positions were supported with artillery. However, Taylor left a third route, a pass farther to the east of the road, foolishly undefended. Taylor held his second brigade in reserve and ordered his third brigade to guard the army's rear.

Santa Anna's men were nearly exhausted by the time they reached the battlefield. He had marched them hard for days. But rather than rest his troops, he hurried to attack the hated Americans. Taylor's men, on the other hand, though outnumbered, were rested and ready to fight.

Santa Anna planned to attack the Americans in three places. He sent two divisions under Generals Santiago Blanco and Francisco Mejia against the two volunteer regiments defending the road to Saltillo. Then he sent two divisions under Generals Manuel Lombardini and Francisco Pacheco to attack the three regiments in the pass. He also sent Pedro de Ampudia, former commander of the Army of the North, into the unguarded pass with two brigades of infantry and cavalry. He held the rest of his army in reserve.

The battle began on the afternoon of February 22. Blanco's men skirmished with the 1st Illinois, but with little effect. Meanwhile, Ampudia's men were progressing unseen through the unguarded pass. An American patrol finally discovered them late in the afternoon, and Taylor sent the 1st Arkansas and 1st Kentucky cavalry regiments to head them off. After several hours of fighting, Ampudia's men were driven back. Believing (incorrectly, as it turned out) that the Mexicans would not try to approach through the pass again, Taylor sent the two American cavalry units to join the three regiments defending the other pass.[2]

The next day, Blanco's men resumed their attack along the road to Saltillo but the 1st Illinois and several batteries of flying artillery repulsed them.

Lombardini's and Pacheco's men, however, managed to route the 2nd Indiana and the two cavalry regiments and outflank the 2nd Illinois. They were breaking through the center of the American line when they were halted temporarily by a furious barrage from several batteries of flying artillery. At the same time, the 1st Mississippi Regiment, commanded by Colonel Jefferson Davis, charged into the gap left by the retreating Americans and rallied the 2nd Indiana. Supported by the flying artillery, the Mississippi volunteers actually forced Lombardini's and Pacheco's divisions to fall back.

Jefferson Davis would become President of the Confederate States of America during the Civil War.

After a brief lull in the fighting, Santa Anna sent a reserve division commanded by General José María Ortega along the same undefended route that Ampudia had followed the day before. Once again, an American patrol discovered the move before Ortega's men could outflank the Americans. They were able to route the Mexicans once again.

By now, the Mexican force seemed exhausted, so Taylor ordered his men to charge. But once the Mexicans saw how few Americans there were, they rallied and returned to the attack. Once again, the Americans fell back, and once again, the flying artillery

This stylized image shows the Americans facing off against the Mexicans at the Battle of Buena Vista. The Americans would emerge the victors from this battle.

saved the day. After several more hours of furious fighting, both sides had had enough. By nightfall, the battlefield was quiet.

The Mexicans had hurt Taylor's small army badly. But the Americans had hurt Santa Anna's larger army even worse.[3]

During the night, Taylor received supplies and reinforcements, and by morning he had as many men and as much ammunition as he had before the Battle of Buena Vista. Santa Anna's army, on the other hand, was worn out and its supplies were just about gone. When morning broke, the Americans discovered that the Mexicans had left. Instead of pursuing them, Taylor marched his army back to Monterrey. It would remain there for the remainder of the war.

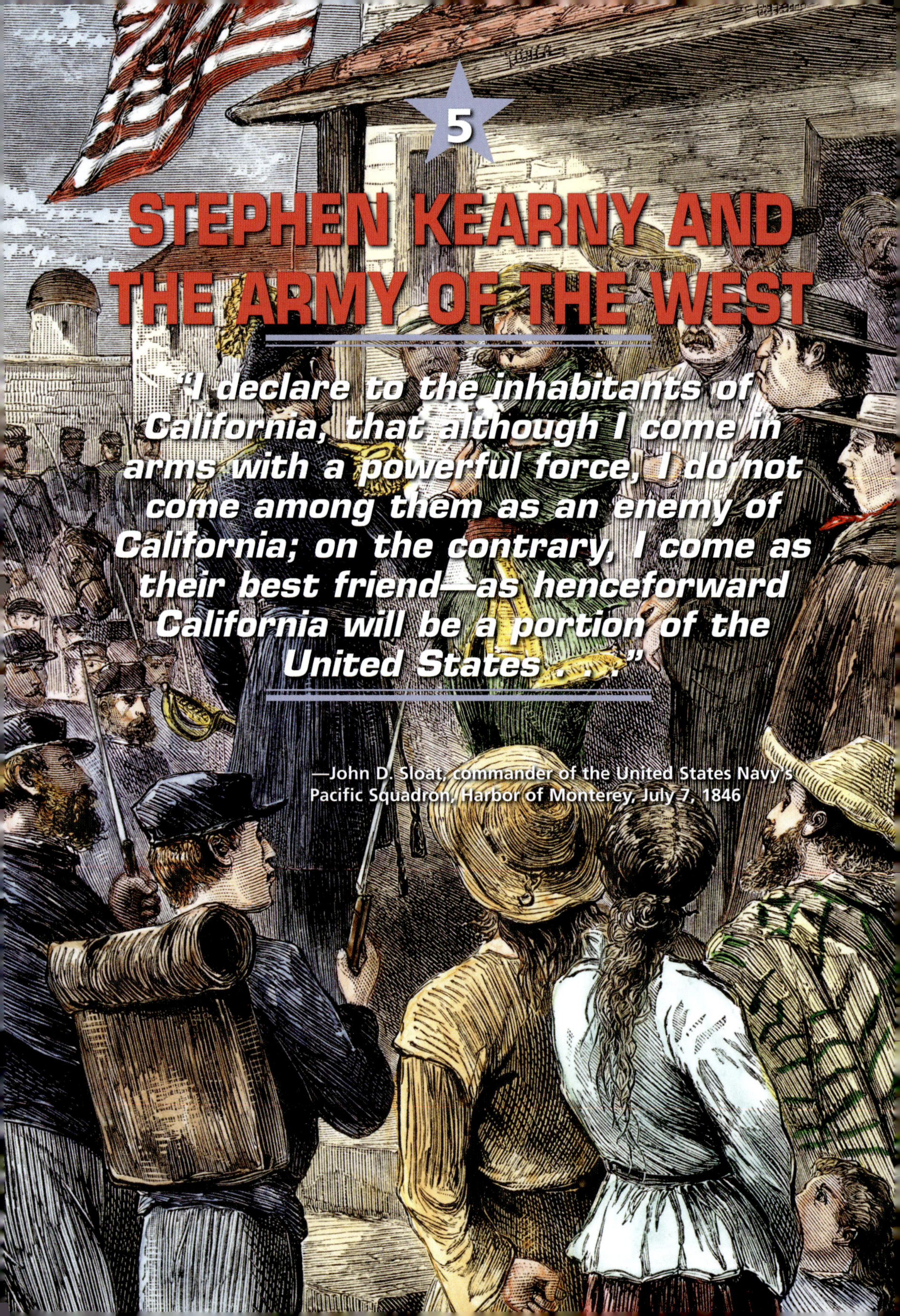

5

STEPHEN KEARNY AND THE ARMY OF THE WEST

"I declare to the inhabitants of California, that although I come in arms with a powerful force, I do not come among them as an enemy of California; on the contrary, I come as their best friend—as henceforward California will be a portion of the United States . . . ."

—John D. Sloat, commander of the United States Navy's Pacific Squadron, Harbor of Monterey, July 7, 1846

While General Zachary Taylor's army invaded north-eastern Mexico, the much smaller Army of the West was campaigning in Nuevo Mexico and Upper California. The territory that Taylor's army captured never became part of the United States, but the western lands that the Army of the West conquered did. Even though this group of American soldiers was small, in the long run its accomplishments would actually be more important to the United States than those of Taylor's army.

Nuevo Mexico

When the Spanish settled there in 1598, Nuevo Mexico was home to perhaps 25,000 American Indians, mostly Pueblo. Over the next 250 years, the Hispanic residents mixed with the Pueblo and built a local economy based on cattle and sheep ranching. The large estates where this ranching took place were located mostly along the Rio Grande, especially near the small towns of Albuquerque and Taos, and around the capital at Santa Fe. A prosperous trade between Santa Fe and Independence, Missouri, was conducted along the Santa Fe Trail by a handful of American traders operating out of Santa Fe. However, few people other than Pueblo, Apache, and Navajo Indians lived in the rest of Nuevo Mexico. It was mostly desert and mountains.

In 1846, Nuevo Mexico's population consisted of slightly more than 50,000 Mexicans, perhaps 30,000 Indians, and approximately 1,000 Americans. These people felt little attachment to the rest of Mexico, partly because their commercial ties were stronger with the United States, and partly because the Mexican government paid little attention to them. The result was a society that felt little loyalty to the federal government in Mexico City over 1,000 miles (1,609 km) away.[1]

The American merchants in Santa Fe wanted Nuevo Mexico to join the United States so they could avoid Mexican trade regulations. They also hoped they would have more control over local affairs than they did under Mexican rule. Also, a growing number of Americans from east of the Mississippi River wanted to relocate to California. The overland trail that ran through Nuevo Mexico stayed open year-round, while trails to its north were impassable during the winter. In addition, Texans claimed the section of Nuevo Mexico east of the Rio Grande as part of their state. For these reasons, Americans wanted Nuevo Mexico for themselves.[2]

On May 13, 1846, the same day Congress declared war against Mexico, President James K. Polk ordered Colonel Stephen W. Kearny to conquer Nuevo Mexico. Kearny was commander of the 1st Dragoons (mounted infantry) Regiment, and he was an excellent choice to lead this expedition. He had spent the last thirty years as an army officer in the West. He probably knew more about the lay of the land and understood American Indians better than any other officer in the United States Army. He also had a reputation for being tough but fair and for being an excellent leader when the going got tough.

Colonel Stephen Kearny led a small army to take control of New Mexico and California and gain more territory for the United States.

In addition to the dragoons, Kearny's force included a regiment of volunteer mounted infantry and three batteries of artillery. The Army of the West, as Colonel Kearny's force was called, totaled 1,600 men.

The Army of the West left Independence, Missouri, in late June 1846. Although the troops followed the Santa Fe Trail almost the entire way, the trip was not easy. It was summer, and very hot, so the men could not find enough grass to feed their hungry animals or enough water to drink. At least sixty horses died during the journey. Fortunately, all the men survived. Kearny's troops finally reached Nuevo Mexico in August, after traveling 900—extremely hot and exhausting— miles (1,448 km).[3]

Meanwhile, the governor of Nuevo Mexico, Manuel Armijo, found out that Kearny's army was approaching. Five years earlier, Armijo had easily defeated a band of Texas volunteers who had come to stake the Republic of Texas's claim over Nuevo Mexico, and Armijo believed that he could defeat Kearny's men, too. But when Armijo tried to raise a defensive force, he discovered that very few Mexicans in this area were willing to fight for Mexico against the United States. When Kearny's men showed up on the outskirts of Santa Fe in mid-August, Armijo had fled to Albuquerque. The locals he left behind offered Kearny no resistance. The battle for Nuevo Mexico was over before it started.[4]

California

Kearny's orders called for him to continue on to California if he thought he could make the trip before winter came. He left behind some men to keep the peace in Santa Fe and Albuquerque, and he sent the Missouri volunteers and about half of the dragoons south to join General Zachary Taylor's army at Monterrey. Then Kearny and the rest of the Army of the West set out for the Pacific Ocean.

In many respects, California was like Nuevo Mexico. Its economy revolved around cattle ranching, and the Mexican citizens lived in just a few places. In addition to the small coastal towns of

Yerba Buena (modern-day San Francisco), Monterey, San Pedro, San Diego, and Los Angeles (the territorial capital), a number of people lived on big ranches in the Sacramento Valley. Trade flourished between these communities and the United States via the Overland Trail, which ran from California to Santa Fe. The rest of the territory was inhabited by American Indians, fur trappers, and miners.[5]

In 1846, California's entire population was slightly more than 25,000. This total included about 15,000 American Indians from a number of tribes as well as approximately 10,000 Californios, the Mexican descendants of the Spanish settlers of the area. California also contained about 1,200 whites of non-Hispanic descent, including about 800 Americans.[6] The Californios' commercial ties were stronger with the United States than with Mexico, and the Mexican government took even less interest in what happened in California than in what happened in Nuevo Mexico. A series of revolutions in the 1840s had made the Mexican government's hold on California so weak, in fact, that the territory was now a semi-independent region.

Unlike the Mexicans in Nuevo Mexico, who did not seem to care if they belonged to Mexico or the United States, the Californios were a fiercely independent group. Most of the Americans living in California wanted it to join the United States, but the Californios strongly opposed this idea. They feared statehood would bring in too many Americans, who would eventually take control of California away from the Californios. So, when American troops tried to take over California, the Californios fought back.[7]

The Bear Flag Republic

By the time Kearny crossed the Colorado River into modern-day California in December, the struggle for California was well under way. In mid-June 1846, a group of about 150 American settlers in the Sacramento Valley formed the California Battalion. Their leader was John C. Frémont, a United States Army captain and surveyor who had been sent to California by the United States government to make maps. Like Kearny, Frémont was a veteran who had spent many years in the West. He commanded a great deal of respect from his men. After defeating a band of poorly organized Californio horsemen, Frémont's followers declared the independence of California from Mexico. Because their flag had a picture of a grizzly bear on it, their "country" was known as the Bear Flag Republic. However, rather than remain independent, the Republic wanted to join the United States as soon as possible.[8]

On July 2, Commodore John D. Sloat, commander of the United States Navy's Pacific Squadron, entered the harbor of Monterey, California, with five ships while on a routine cruise. When he heard about the creation of the Bear Flag Republic, he landed 250 marines and sailors and took control of Monterey. He also sent a force to capture Yerba Buena. Now that they had the support of the United States military, the California Battalion declared California a loyal territory of the United States.

On July 23, Sloat was relieved by Commodore Robert F. Stockton. Stockton was an energetic veteran of the United States Navy and a man with a reputation for being quite resourceful when the occasion demanded. This was fortunate for the Americans, because now the occasion demanded that Stockton take command of all the units fighting in California under the American flag.

Commodore Stockton immediately sent the California Battalion to capture San Diego from another Californio militia force and sent about 300 marines and sailors to capture Los Angeles. In both places, the Californios offered little resistance. However, not all Californios had given up. They were just waiting for the right moment to attack. That moment came when the California Battalion returned to the Sacramento Valley and Stockton returned to Monterey. Led by Captain José María Flores, in late September, 300 Californios rose up and ran the Americans out of Los Angeles and San Diego. When an American force of 400 marines and sailors tried to retake Los Angeles, Flores's men ran them off as well. By the time Kearny arrived in California in December, the Californios controlled the southern half of California and the Americans controlled the northern half.[9]

Kearny Versus the Californios

On December 5, Kearny was joined by some of Stockton's men in the Valley of San Pasqual, just west of the Colorado River. The next day, they ran into a large force of Californio cavalrymen blocking the way out of the valley. Although they were outnumbered and no longer had any horses, Kearny decided to attack anyway. It was a bad decision. Some of the Californios pretended to retreat, and when Kearny's men chased them, the rest of the Californios surrounded and attacked the Americans.

Eighteen Americans died and another thirteen were wounded in this encounter, known as the Battle of San Pasqual.

Kearny's men retreated to a rocky hilltop but, once again, the Californios surrounded them. This time, however, the Americans' position was too difficult to attack. Instead, the Californios kept the Americans from leaving their hilltop to look for food and water. After five days, Kearny's men were desperately hungry and thirsty. They were getting ready to attempt a breakout attack when a large force of American marines and sailors under Stockton's command miraculously arrived and saved Kearny's men.[10]

Commodore Robert F. Stockton helped Captain Frémont and Colonel Kearny take over California.

The Army of the West continued its long march until it reached San Diego, which Stockton's men had already recaptured. For three weeks, Kearny's exhausted dragoons rested while he drilled the sailors into respectable soldiers. Then the 300-man force, this time under the command of Stockton, marched on Los Angeles. On January 8, 1847, 450 mounted Californios attacked the Americans 12 miles (19 km) from Los Angeles at the San Gabriel River. The American infantry easily repulsed several cavalry charges with the help of the artillery, and eventually, the Californios were forced to retreat. This action, known as the Battle of San Gabriel, resulted in fourteen

American casualties. The Californios probably suffered over one hundred casualties.

California's state flag borrowed its design from the Bear Flag Republic's flag.

The next day, the Americans continued their march on Los Angeles. Once again, the Californios attacked them, this time at La Mesa on the outskirts of Los Angeles. And once again, the American artillery was able to disperse them. On January 10, 1847, the Americans entered Los Angeles. By this time, the Californios realized that further resistance was useless. The struggle for California was finally over. A major portion of the land that Americans had wanted under Manifest Destiny had been acquired by the efforts of a relatively small band of men.[11]

6

WINFIELD SCOTT AND THE ARMY OF THE EAST

"HURRAH FOR OLD KENTUCK! THAT'S THE WAY TO DO IT."

—Zachary Taylor shouting to the 2nd Kentucky Regiment on seeing them rally in battle at Buena Viata, Mexico, on February 23, 1847.

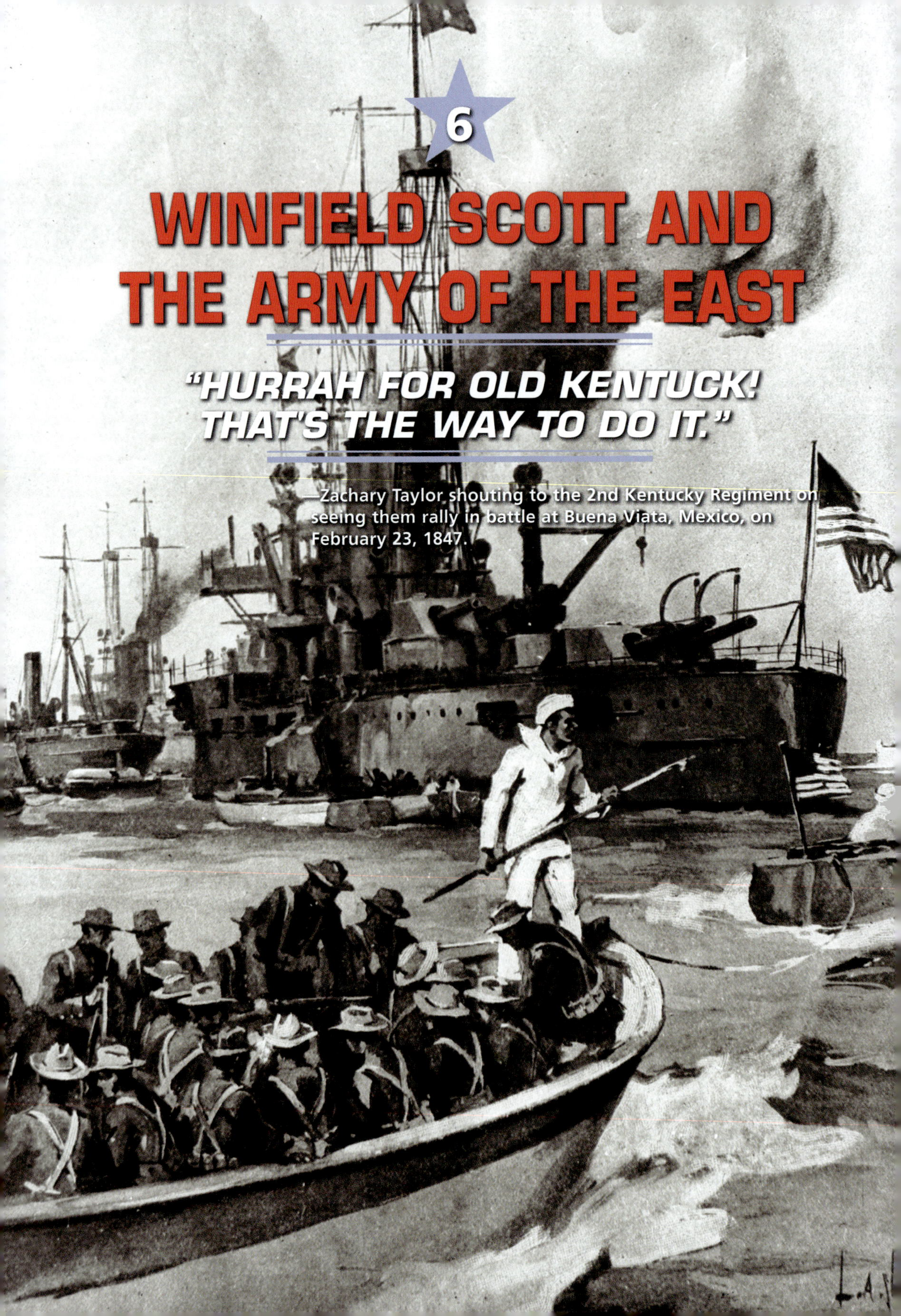

After the Battle of Monterrey, President James K. Polk and General Winfield Scott became convinced that General Zachary Taylor's Army of Occupation would not be able to capture Mexico City by marching south from Monterrey. So they devised a new plan. Scott would land a second army at Veracruz on the Gulf of Mexico and march west to Mexico City.

In terms of personality, Scott was the opposite of Taylor. Taylor liked to wear old dowdy clothes, but Scott loved to dress in fancy uniforms.

Taylor had an "aw shucks" style of speaking, but Scott spoke in a very melodramatic way. A Boston newspaper once wrote that Scott "acts like a god and talks like a fool."[1] Scott was so particular about every little thing being done exactly the right way that his troops called him "Old Fuss and Feathers." But in terms of military leadership, Scott was as good a general as Taylor, maybe even better.[2]

Scott's plan to end the war was a good one for several reasons. First, Veracruz is only about 200 miles (322 km) from Mexico City. This is about one third the distance between Monterrey, where Taylor was, and the Mexican capital. Second, Veracruz was connected to Mexico City by a good road called the National Highway. This road was much better than the ones on which Taylor would have to travel. Third, the United States Navy could supply and reinforce Scott's army through Veracruz. His supply lines would never be longer than 200 miles (322 km). Taylor's supply lines, on the other hand, were already stretched much too thin.

General Winfield Scott was General-in-Chief of the United States Army during the war with Mexico.

However, there were two major problems with Scott's plan. Veracruz was heavily fortified and the Mexicans would almost certainly oppose any landing there. And in order for the landing to work, Scott estimated that he needed 12,000 men, fifty large transport ships to carry them, and 140 small landing craft to get them from ship to shore. So, in order for Scott's plan to work, he would have to conduct the largest amphibious landing that the world had ever seen.

Veracruz

As it turned out, the landing was easier to execute than anyone predicted. The biggest problem was getting all the ships and landing craft together in the same place at the same time. This problem was neatly solved by the army's Quartermaster General, Thomas S. Jesup. Since the United States military had no troop transport ships, Jesup simply chartered enough merchant ships to carry Scott's troops. In New Orleans, Jesup supervised the construction of surfboats designed by Lieutenant George M. Totten to carry the troops from the ships to the beach.[3]

Scott's army of 8,000 volunteers and 4,000 regulars left Lobos Island on March 2. After a week at sea, the troops began landing on March 9. Rather than assault Veracruz directly from the shore under the guns of the city's forts, Scott decided to land his men on Collada Beach, about 2 miles (3.2 km) south of Veracruz. Except for a few rounds fired from the guns of one of the forts, the Mexicans did not offer much resistance.

Rather than attack Veracruz with his infantry, Scott decided to surround the city and then bombard it with artillery. He had his men dig a trench around Veracruz from Collada Beach to Vergara, about 2 miles (3.2 km) north of the city. This trench was just out of range of the guns in the city's forts. Then he had his men set up the heavy artillery behind the trench and begin shelling the city. For five days, the American guns pounded Veracruz mercilessly. Finally, on March 27, the 5,000-man Mexican garrison surrendered. Scott and his men had pulled off one of the most ambitious military undertakings to date and made it look easy. The road to Mexico City, and victory, now seemed to be wide open for the Americans.[4]

Cerro Gordo

While Scott's army besieged Veracruz, General Antonio López de Santa Anna's army was moving south to intercept it. But before he could do that, he had to rebuild his army again, because many of his troops had deserted after the Battle of Buena Vista. By gathering conscripts, local militias, and national guardsmen, Santa Anna was able to build his force. Called the Army of the East because it was headed to fight in eastern Mexico, it had 12,000 men.[5]

As Scott marched his army up the National Highway from Veracruz, Santa Anna's army hurried down the National Highway from Mexico City. Santa Anna planned to defend the road at a mountain pass east of the village of Cerro Gordo, about 50 miles (80 km) west of Veracruz. It was a good place for a defending army. Steep hills overlooked the National Highway on both sides. To the south of the road ran the Del Plan River, which made Santa Anna's right flank even more secure. To the north of the road were many gullies and much thick chaparral. Attacking from this angle would be very difficult for the Americans. To the east of the pass were three cliffs from which artillery could pound anything moving up the road. Santa Anna placed his artillery on these cliffs, the bulk of his troops in the hills, and held the rest of his men he placed in reserve in Cerro Gordo.

Advance scouts of both armies skirmished on April 11, and the Americans came to a halt. Although the Mexican position looked unbeatable, American engineers found a narrow path through the gullies and chaparral to the north of the Mexican position that eventually came out behind the Mexican lines. Scott decided to have his engineers widen the path so he could send the main attack along this path. Meanwhile, the rest of the army would distract the artillery to the east of the pass to give the engineers time.

For six days, American engineers widened the path. Then, on April 17, Scott sent a division commanded by General David E. Twiggs down the path while the rest of the army created a diversion by attacking the Mexican artillery positions on the cliffs. Twiggs's men got past the Mexican artillery without being seen. Before they could bypass the main body of Mexican troops, however, they were spotted and attacked. After a full day of fierce fighting, Twiggs's advance was halted.[6]

On April 18, Scott sent a second division commanded by General William J. Worth, whose men had fought so well at Monterrey, to reinforce Twiggs. While their two divisions turned off the path to attack the left flank of the Mexican position, General James Shields's brigade of three hundred men continued down the path and got completely around the Mexican position. His men made it all the way to the National Highway at Cerro Gordo where they ran into Santa Anna's reserves—about 2,000 men. These troops forced Shields's men to retreat back down the path.

But while Santa Anna's reserves were repulsing the American surprise attack, the rest of the Army of the East heard that a large part of the American Army had bypassed their main position. This report threw the Mexicans into a panic. Thinking that thousands of Americans would soon be surrounding them, many Mexican soldiers began to flee. Before long the entire Army of the East was retreating as fast as it could. Santa Anna himself left the field so quickly that some Illinois volunteers were able to capture Santa Anna's personal carriage. In it was one of his spare wooden legs.[7]

The Battle of Cerro Gordo was a major disaster for the Mexicans. While American casualties were about 400 killed and wounded, more than 1,000 Mexicans were killed or wounded and over 3,000 were taken prisoner. The army that Santa Anna had worked so hard to rebuild was shattered. What was left of it retreated all the way back to Mexico City. Worst of all, the Mexican Army had failed again to defeat a smaller American force. Many Mexicans began to wonder if they ever would.[8]

Keeping the Troops Supplied

After resting for two weeks in Jalapa, just 4 miles (6.4 km) west of Cerro Gordo, Scott's army resumed its westward march. On May 15, it entered Puebla, about 75 miles (121 km) east of Mexico City, without a fight. Here the Americans rested for three months. During this time, Scott was reinforced with a large number of volunteers so that his army now contained 14,000 men. Partly because of these

Santa Anna's wooden leg was captured by an Illinois infantry regiment. It is on display in the Illinois State Military Museum.

reinforcements, he had to solve a major supply problem facing his army.

As Scott's army pushed further inland, it became clear that keeping the troops supplied would not be as easy as Polk and Scott had hoped. The Americans did not have enough wagons and mules to keep supplies moving on a regular basis from Veracruz to the front lines. Also, Mexican guerrillas harassed the American wagon trains so much that they required heavy armed escorts. Scott's men were already outnumbered, and Scott was afraid that using some men as escorts would make the army too weak to capture Mexico City.[9]

7

FIGHTING FOR MEXICO CITY

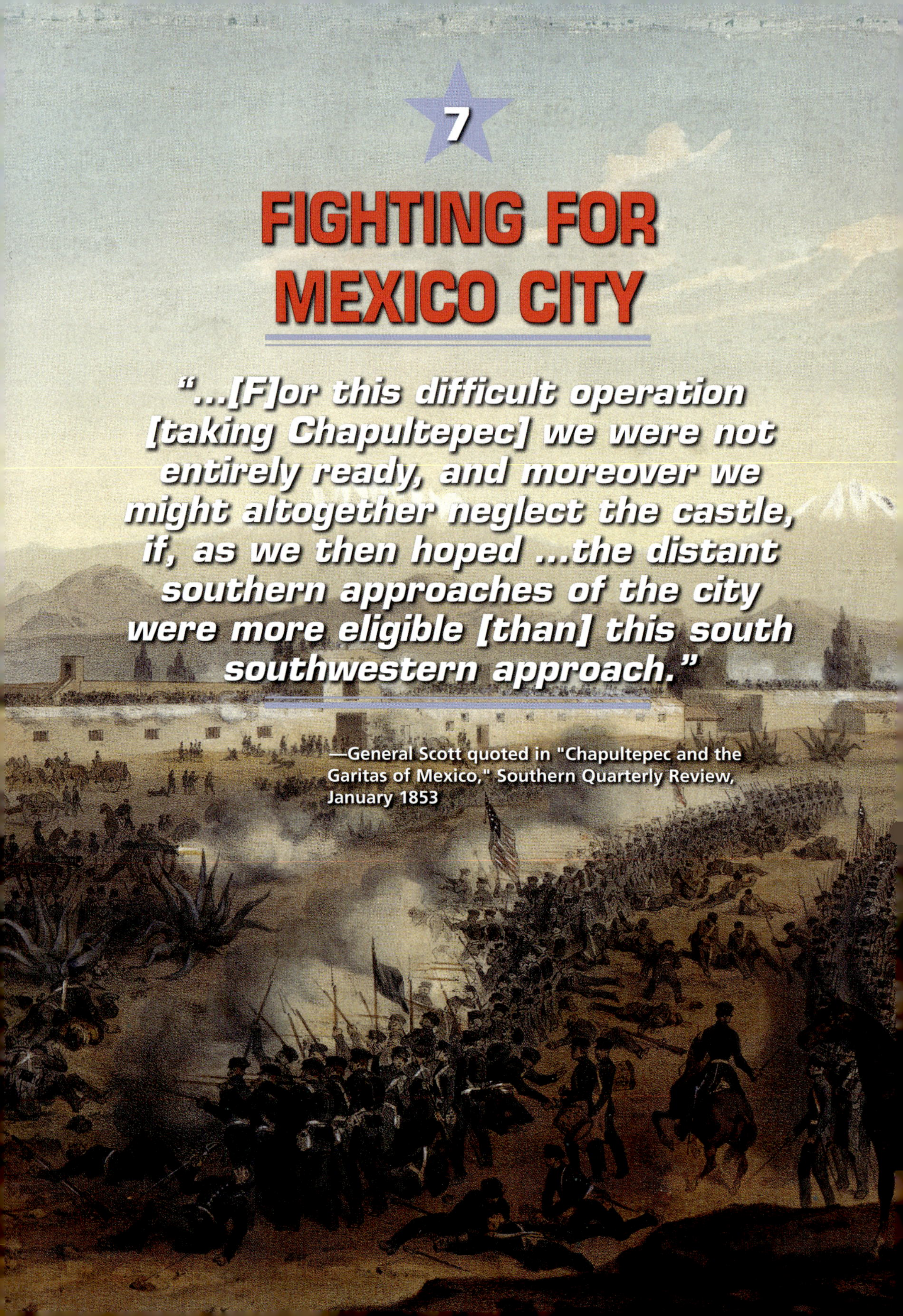

"...[F]or this difficult operation [taking Chapultepec] we were not entirely ready, and moreover we might altogether neglect the castle, if, as we then hoped ...the distant southern approaches of the city were more eligible [than] this south southwestern approach."

—General Scott quoted in "Chapultepec and the Garitas of Mexico," Southern Quarterly Review, January 1853

So Scott decided to stop worrying about his supply lines. Ammunition, of course, would still have to be transported by wagon train, but from now on, his army would live off the land. Every day, a number of American troops would be sent out into the countryside and local marketplaces to round up enough cattle, chickens, corn, beans, and water to fill the army's needs for the next day. This plan was a daring gamble, because Scott did not know for sure that he would find enough food.

However, living off the land would make it possible for his army to get to Mexico City faster, where he hoped to end the war by winning a huge victory.[1]

While General Winfield Scott rested in Puebla, General Antonio López de Santa Anna busied himself raising a defensive army for the third time that year. He salvaged 3,500 men from the remains of the Army of the East, rounded up another 4,000 stragglers from the remains of the old Army of the North, and called in General Juan Alvarez's 2,500-man Army of the South, which had been harassing Scott's supply lines. To these men Santa Anna added 10,000 militiamen and 10,000 recruits he was able to round up in and around Mexico City. By the time he was done, he had an army of 30,000 men, more than twice the number the American Army had.[2]

On August 7, Scott's army of four divisions began marching west from Puebla to Mexico City. It met little resistance before reaching the pass that carries

Pedregal *means "rocky ground" in Spanish.*

the National Highway over the mountains to the east of the Valley of Mexico, which was the heartland of the old Aztec Empire. From the pass, Scott's men could see the Mexican capital and the three lovely lakes to the south.[3]

Scott had intended to attack Mexico City from the east. He changed his mind when he discovered that the National Highway was heavily defended 25 miles (40 km) east of the city at a mountain called El Penon. Instead, he decided to go around El Penon by taking a branch of the National Highway that approached the capital from the south.

Around 8 miles (13 km) south of Mexico City, Scott's army encountered an unusual geologic formation known as the Pedregal. The Pedregal is a field of solid lava that had been deposited over thousands of years by a nearby volcano, Mount Zacatepec. The lava is so hard, sharp and jagged that it was impossible for Scott's army to cross it. Fortunately, the branch of the National Highway they were following skirts the Pedregal to the east. But when Scott discovered that the Mexican Army was blocking his way at the village of San Antonio, he had to come up with another plan.

Scott decided to leave the division commanded by General William J. Worth just outside San Antonio to keep an eye on the Mexicans there. Then he sent the two divisions commanded by Generals David E. Twiggs and Gideon J. Pillow along a narrow trail that skirts the Pedregal to the west. The idea was for Twiggs and Pillow to come in behind the Mexicans at San Antonio and attack them from the rear while Worth attacked from the front.

Padierna/Contreras

On August 19, before they could reach San Antonio, Twiggs and Pillow ran into a Mexican force at the village of Padierna. This force was commanded by General Gabriel Valencia and contained 5,000 men, about the same as the two American division combined. The two sides exchanged shots throughout the day. Late in the afternoon, some of the Americans managed to sneak around the Mexican left flank, and by the time dark had fallen they had gotten behind Valencia's main position. The Americans thought they had Valencia's men surrounded, and they did. But then they made a sickening discovery; Santa Anna's main army was only 2 miles (3.2 km) away, and a good number of Americans were now trapped between it and Valencia's force.[4]

Had Santa Anna attacked in the morning with the main body of his army, he probably would have destroyed the two American divisions. Almost certainly, this would have destroyed Scott's army and ended the war in Mexico's favor. Instead, Santa Anna retreated to the north toward Mexico City, leaving Valencia's men to fight the Americans alone. No one knows for sure why Santa Anna did this. The most likely reason is that he hated Valencia, who was one of his most bitter political rivals. In 1844, Valencia had helped remove Santa Anna from the Mexican presidency and exiled him from the country. Perhaps Santa Anna abandoned Valencia to the Americans as a way of getting revenge. Whatever the reason, the Americans benefited greatly from this piece of luck. Instead of being routed by the combined forces of

Santa Anna and Valencia on the morning of August 20, the Americans attacked and defeated Valencia's men in Padierna. The Battle of Contreras, as the Americans called it, lasted twenty minutes. Seven hundred Mexicans were killed and another 800 taken prisoner. The Americans suffered only 60 killed and wounded.[5]

Churubusco

After the defeat, Valencia's men and the defenders at San Antonio fell back to the village of Churubusco on the Churubusco River. This river is too wide and deep to wade, and so the only way for Scott's army to cross it was at a bridge. Santa Anna knew this, and so he ordered the rest of his army to Churubusco as well to defend the bridge that carried the National Highway from San Antonio to Mexico City.[6]

At this point, Scott made a mistake that could have been costly. Instead of trying to cross the river at two smaller bridges to the west of Churubusco, which were lightly defended, he decided to force his way across the National Highway bridge. The odds clearly seemed to be against the Americans, who had 2,600 attackers against about 8,000 Mexican defenders. However, the Mexicans were by now tired, hungry, and demoralized from their earlier defeat that day. In fact, the entire war now seemed like a nightmare to most of the Mexican troops. It seemed that no matter how bravely they fought, they would always manage to find a way to lose. Even though they still outnumbered the Americans and would continue to fight bravely, very few

Mexican soldiers actually still expected to beat the hated Yankees.

For about two hours, bullets flew hot and heavy, with neither side giving an inch. Finally, the superior discipline and confidence of the Americans turned the tide of battle. Despite being outnumbered, they fixed bayonets and charged, causing the Mexicans to break and run away.

The Battles of Padierna/Contreras and Churubusco, both of which were fought on August 20, were costly for both sides. The Americans lost more than 100 killed and almost 1,000 wounded.The Mexicans, on the other hand, lost 4,000 killed and wounded, while another 3,000 were captured. Although Scott's army suffered heavy losses, Santa Anna's army had been destroyed.[7]

Santa Anna immediately sent word to Scott, asking for a truce while a peace treaty could be worked out. On August 22, Scott agreed. He knew that any peace treaty signed at this point would probably give the Americans just about everything they wanted without having to lose any more men in battle. But before the peace talks could even begin, Santa Anna violated the truce by building up the fortifications around Mexico City. On September 7, Scott began planning for the final attack of the war, this time on the Mexican capital.[8]

Mexico City

Mexico City sat in the middle of a marshy plain that was too wet for an army to march over. Therefore, Scott planned to take the capital by marching from the south and west along several causeways. These long, built-up mounds of earth carried roads across the marshy plain into Mexico City. The approaches to the western causeways were defended by three imposing structures. Molino del Rey was a group of stone buildings about 200 yards (183 m) in length. Casa Mata was a large stone building 500 yards (457 m) west of Molino del Rey. And the Castle of Chapultepec was a fortified castle on top of a hill about 1,000 yards (914 m) east of Molino del Rey.

Scott knew that attacking these three forts would be just as difficult for him as attacking the strongpoints north of Monterrey had been for Zachary Taylor. But Scott also knew that his men had overcome many difficulties already, and he believed that they could overcome this one as well. He could have bypassed these three forts, but that would have left a number of the enemy in strong defensive positions to his rear, something no army commander ever wants to do. And so, Scott gave the order to take the three forts.[9]

On the morning of September 8, 1847, Scott sent Worth's division to attack Molino del Rey. The Mexican defenders fought bravely but they were quickly outnumbered and surrounded. After about an hour of fierce fighting, they were forced to surrender. Then, Worth's men turned their attention to Casa Mata. An artillery barrage, followed by a bayonet charge, succeeded in making its Mexican defenders flee, but at great cost to the Americans. Between the two engagements, Worth's men had more than 100 killed and almost 700 wounded.

The battle for Chapultepec was the crucial one. Casualties were wearing down Scott's army rapidly,

Not only were its walls tall and strong, but Chapultepec Castle also sat atop a hill, making the attack on the castle all the more challenging.

and the Americans could not afford any more costly victories like the ones at Molino del Rey and Casa Mata. Not only did the Americans have to take the castle, but they had to take it without suffering very many losses. However, its steep walls were 200 feet (61 m) high. The only way in would be to storm the main gate or scale the walls on ladders. Both of these options were dangerous missions for any soldier. Many Americans felt sure they could not capture Chapultepec no matter how many of them died in the attempt.[10]

The battle for Chapultepec began on the morning of September 12 with a massive artillery barrage. Scott hoped that this would make Chapultepec's 250 defenders surrender.

The next morning, the storming and scaling parties were sent into action. Fortunately for the Americans, they were able to send up fifty scaling parties at the same time. By this time, there were not enough Mexicans left to defend against all fifty scaling parties. It was only a matter of time before the American attackers began pouring over the walls. Despite fierce fighting, Chapultepec fell to the Americans after only two hours. When the number of killed and wounded was counted at the end of the day, the Americans had suffered four hundred fifty casualties.[11]

Chapultepec's fall opened the doors of Mexico City to the Americans. While the exhausted Americans rested during the night, Santa Anna retreated from Mexico City with what was left of his army. On September 14, General Winfield Scott rode into the capital's Grand Plaza at the head of his crippled but victorious army.

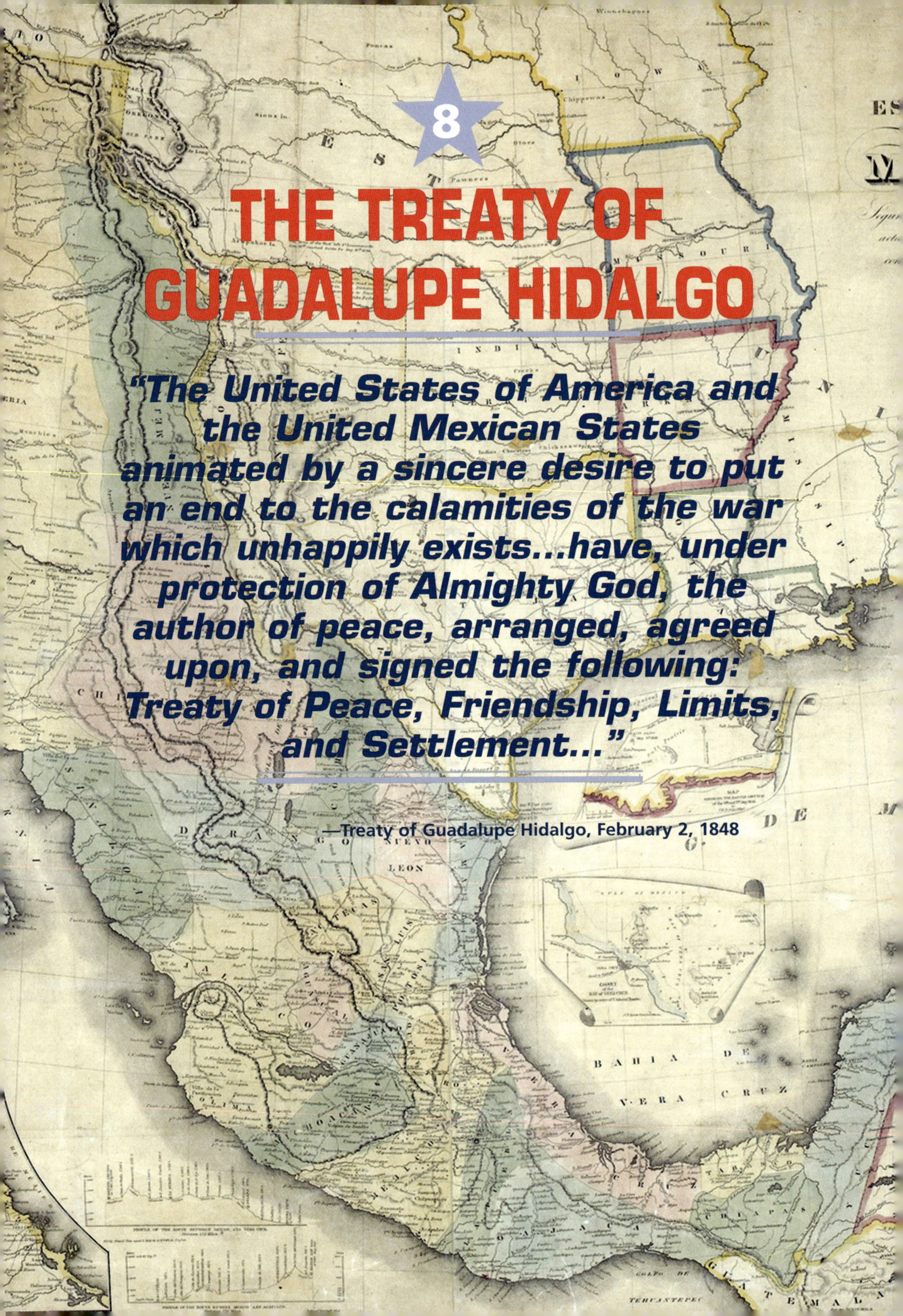

8

THE TREATY OF GUADALUPE HIDALGO

"The United States of America and the United Mexican States animated by a sincere desire to put an end to the calamities of the war which unhappily exists...have, under protection of Almighty God, the author of peace, arranged, agreed upon, and signed the following: Treaty of Peace, Friendship, Limits, and Settlement..."

—Treaty of Guadalupe Hidalgo, February 2, 1848

No war ends just because the fighting stops, and the Mexican-American War was no exception. Even though General Winfield Scott had destroyed Santa Anna's army and captured Mexico City, it remained to be seen exactly what the Americans had won and what the Mexicans had lost. All these details were worked out in the peace treaty that brought the war to a close, the Treaty of Guadalupe Hidalgo. The American most responsible for bringing about the treaty was not a soldier but a statesman, Nicholas P. Trist.

Trist was the chief clerk of the State Department, and he seemed to be the perfect man to work out a peace treaty with the Mexicans. He had been a cadet at the United States Military Academy at West Point. He had been a law student of former President Thomas Jefferson and a private secretary to former President Andrew Jackson. More importantly, he was an intelligent and charming person, he spoke Spanish fluently, and he had served as consul (a type of junior ambassador) in Havana, Cuba. On April 10, 1847, two weeks after Scott's army captured Veracruz, President James K. Polk sent Nicholas Trist to Mexico to see if he could work out a peaceful settlement to the war with the Mexican government.[1]

Nicholas Trist served as ambassador to Mexico. He was sent to negotiate a treaty with the defeated Mexican government that would win territory for the United States.

Trist's first attempts to make peace did not work out very well. Shortly after the Battle of Cerro Gordo, Santa Anna, who was also the president of Mexico, approached Trist. Santa Anna offered to surrender, thus ending the war, in return for a bribe of $1 million, with $10,000 to be paid in advance as a sign of the Americans' good faith. With the approval of Scott, Trist decided to take up Santa Anna on the offer and paid him the $10,000 in the hopes this would bring a quick and painless end to the war. But the Mexican general was just playing the Americans for fools; he kept the money but never talked to Trist about making peace. Accepting defeat on this one, Trist next sent a note to Jose Ramon Pacheco, the Mexican foreign minister, requesting a meeting so they could talk about making peace, but Pacheco just ignored him.[2]

Shortly thereafter, Pacheco was replaced by Manuel de la Peña y Peña, and he agreed to open talks with Trist. But before they could make much progress, Trist received a letter from President Polk telling him to come home. The president was afraid that Trist's mission was leading the Mexicans to think that the Americans were ready to stop fighting and give up on their goals of attaining Mexican territories, which they weren't. But before Trist could leave Mexico, Peña convinced him to stay. The Mexican minister could see that the war was going badly for his country and he was convinced that he would soon have to beg the Americans for peace, something that he did not want to do. So he assured Trist that, if he stayed, they could work out a peace treaty in no time at all.[3]

Although the treaty did not come about quite as fast as Peña had promised, both sides began talking seriously about peace for the first time. In terms of territory, the Mexicans agreed to sell California and New Mexico to the United States. They also agreed that the new boundary between Mexico and the United States would be the Rio Grande from the Gulf of Mexico to the 32nd parallel, about 30 miles (48 km) north of the present-day border between New Mexico and the Mexican state of Chihuahua. The boundary would then run due west until it hit the Gila River, and then follow the river all the way to the Colorado River. Then it would follow the present-day border between California and the Mexican state of Baja California Norte. The lands to

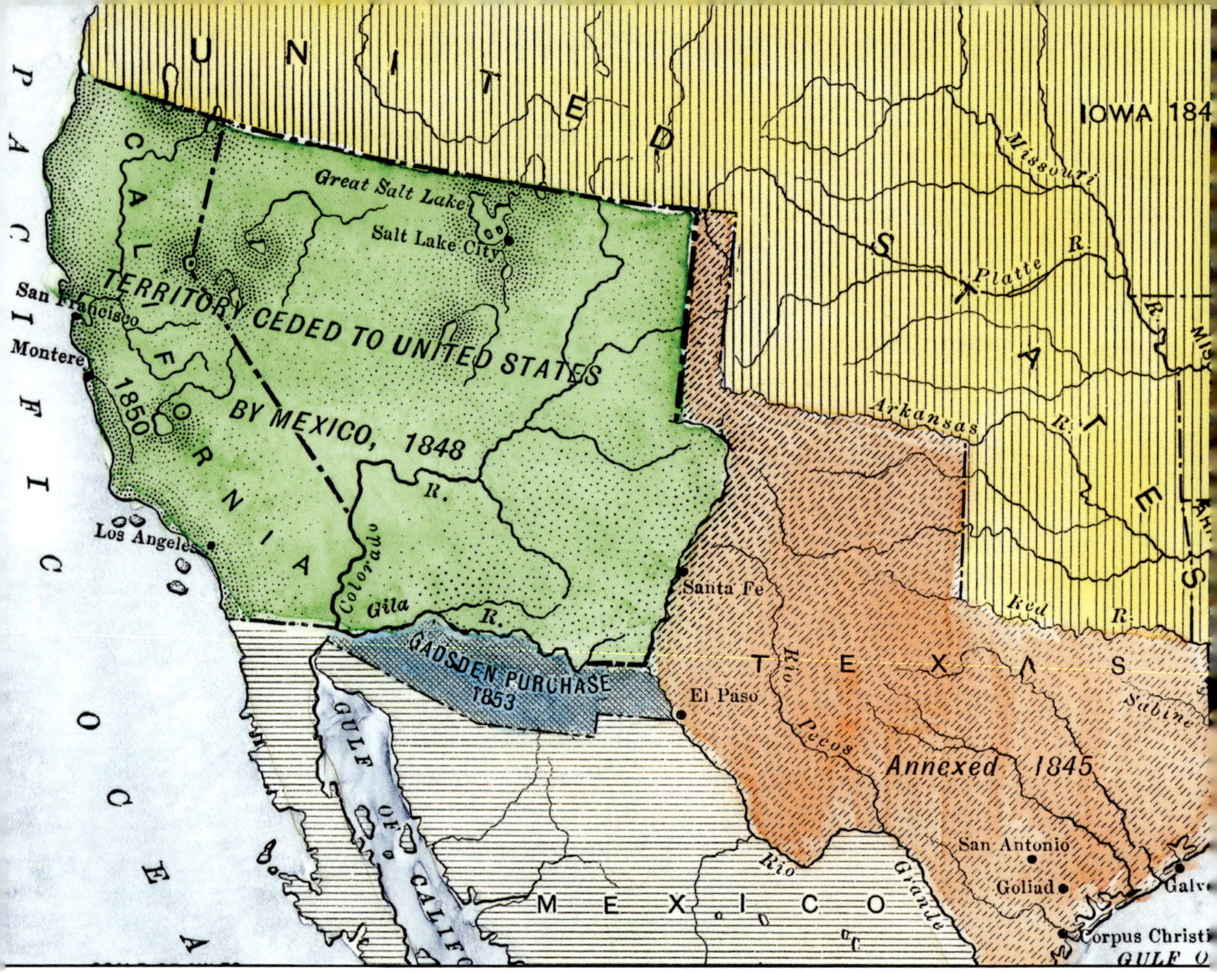

The green area shows the land ceded to America with the Treaty of Guadalupe Hidalgo.

be given up by Mexico became known as the Mexican Cession.

The biggest problem the peace negotiators faced involved money. The Mexicans demanded that the United States pay $30 million for California and New Mexico, an amount Trist could not agree to. Though this was the amount the United States had once offered for these territories, they now had Mexico over a barrel after winning the war. Finally, both sides agreed on a payment of $15 million, with the provision that the United States would also assume

Mexico's debts to the residents in California and New Mexico once the fighting had stopped.[4]

One important article in the Treaty of Guadalupe Hidalgo included provisions for the Mexican citizens living in the lands ceded to the United States. These people could retain their Mexican citizenship if they wanted to without having to move, or to give up their property. They could also choose to be American citizens with all the rights that entailed. If they chose, they could give up their lands and move to Mexico without having to pay any sort of tax or penalty to do so.

Another important article in the treaty made the United States responsible for controlling the American Indians who lived in the Mexican Cession. For centuries, these Indians had been raiding farms and ranches all across northern Mexico, killing men and enslaving women and children. Now, it would be up to the United States to prevent these Native Americans from raiding south from the Mexican Cession into Mexico.[5]

On February 2, 1848, in the town of Guadalupe Hidalgo just outside Mexico City, Trist and the Mexican peace commissioners ended the Mexican-American War by signing the Treaty of Guadalupe Hidalgo. Now the treaty would have to be ratified by the Senates of both the United States and Mexico in order to become official.

Many American senators were unhappy with the Treaty of Guadalupe Hidalgo. Some thought the treaty was too generous to the Mexicans. Others thought the treaty was actually unfair to the Mexicans. A number of senators opposed the treaty simply because Trist had written and signed it after

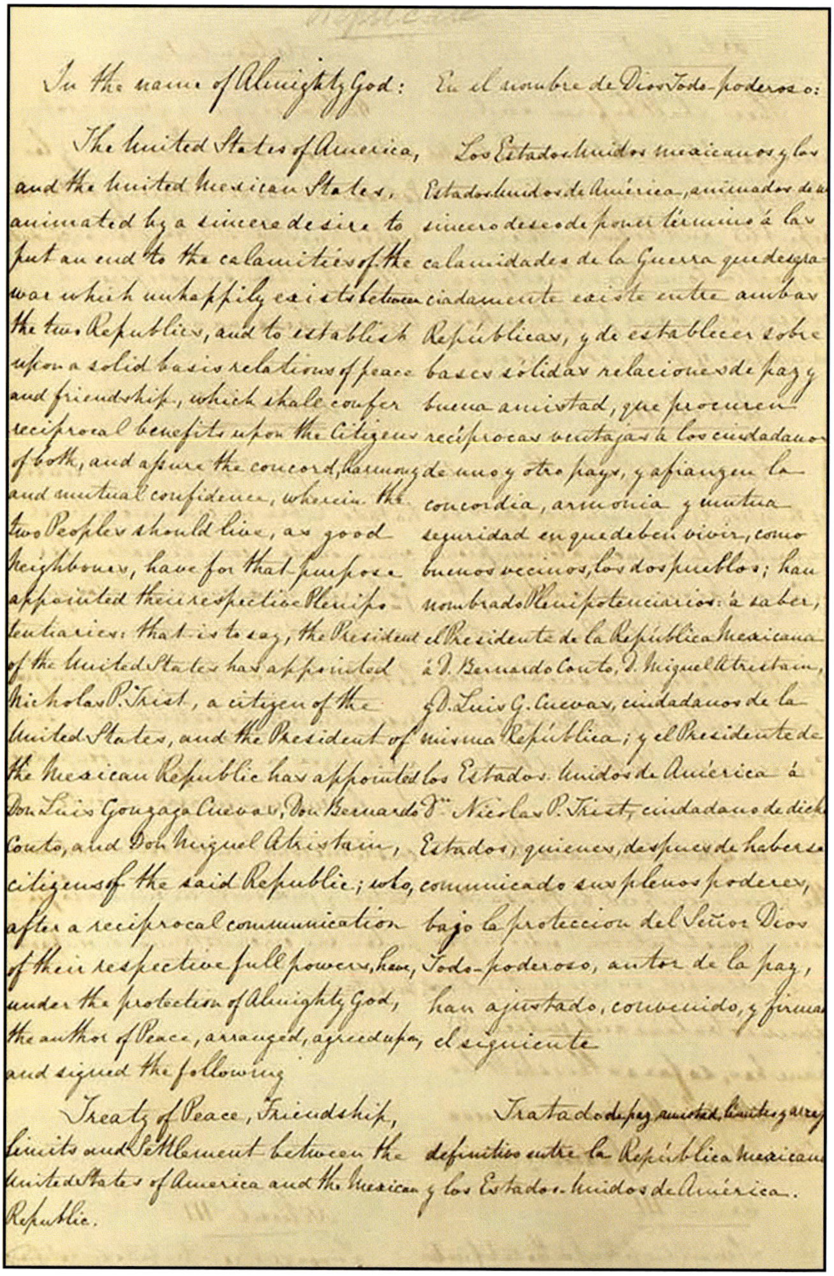

In the name of Almighty God:

The United States of America, and the United Mexican States, animated by a sincere desire to put an end to the calamities of the war which unhappily exists between the two Republics, and to establish upon a solid basis relations of peace and friendship, which shall confer reciprocal benefits upon the citizens of both, and assure the concord, harmony and mutual confidence, wherein the two Peoples should live, as good Neighbours, have for that purpose appointed their respective Plenipotentiaries: that is to say, the President of the United States has appointed Nicholas P. Trist, a citizen of the United States, and the President of the Mexican Republic has appointed Don Luis Gonzaga Cuevas, Don Bernardo Couto, and Don Miguel Atristain, citizens of the said Republic; who, after a reciprocal communication of their respective full powers, have, under the protection of Almighty God, the author of Peace, arranged, agreed upon, and signed the following

Treaty of Peace, Friendship, Limits and Settlement between the United States of America and the Mexican Republic.

En el nombre de Dios Todo-poderoso:

Los Estados Unidos Mexicanos y los Estados Unidos de América, animados de un sincero deseo de poner término á las calamidades de la Guerra que desgraciadamente existe entre ambas Repúblicas, y de establecer sobre bases sólidas relaciones de paz y buena amistad, que procuren recíprocas ventajas á los ciudadanos de uno y otro pays, y afianzen la concordia, armonía y mutua seguridad en que deben vivir, como buenos vecinos, los dos pueblos; han nombrado Plenipotenciarios: á saber, el Presidente de la República Mexicana á D. Bernardo Couto, D. Miguel Atristain, y D. Luis G. Cuevas, ciudadanos de la misma República; y el Presidente de los Estados Unidos de América á D.n Nicolas P. Trist, ciudadano de dichos Estados; quienes, despues de haberse comunicado sus plenos poderes, bajo la proteccion del Señor Dios Todo-poderoso, autor de la paz, han ajustado, convenido, y firmado el siguiente

Tratado de paz, amistad, límites y arreglo definitivo entre la República Mexicana y los Estados Unidos de América.

This is the Treaty of Guadalupe Hidalgo, signed on February 2, 1848.

his authority to do so had been revoked by President Polk.[6]

Polk was furious that Trist had disobeyed his orders but, in the end, he realized that the Treaty of Guadalupe Hidalgo gave the United States about as much as it could expect to get without more fighting. He was able to persuade a majority of the senators to see this, too. On March 10, 1848, the United States Senate ratified the treaty.

The debate in the Mexican Senate was not quite as lengthy. No Mexican senator was happy about giving up California and New Mexico, but all of them realized that, if the war continued, Mexico might lose even more territory. So on March 25, the Mexican Senate also ratified the treaty. The Mexican-American War had finally come to an end. And with that end, the United States had gained all the territory it had hoped to win with its aggressive policy of Manifest Destiny.[7]

9

MEXICO AFTER THE WAR

"What is this territory, Mr. President, which you propose to wrest from Mexico? It is consecrated to the heart of the Mexican by many a well-fought battle with his old Castilian master. His Bunker Hills, and Saratogas, and Yorktowns, are there! The Mexican can say, "There I bled for liberty! and shall I surrender that confiscated home of my affections to the Anglo-Saxon invaders? . . ."

—US Senator Thomas Corwin addressing Congress

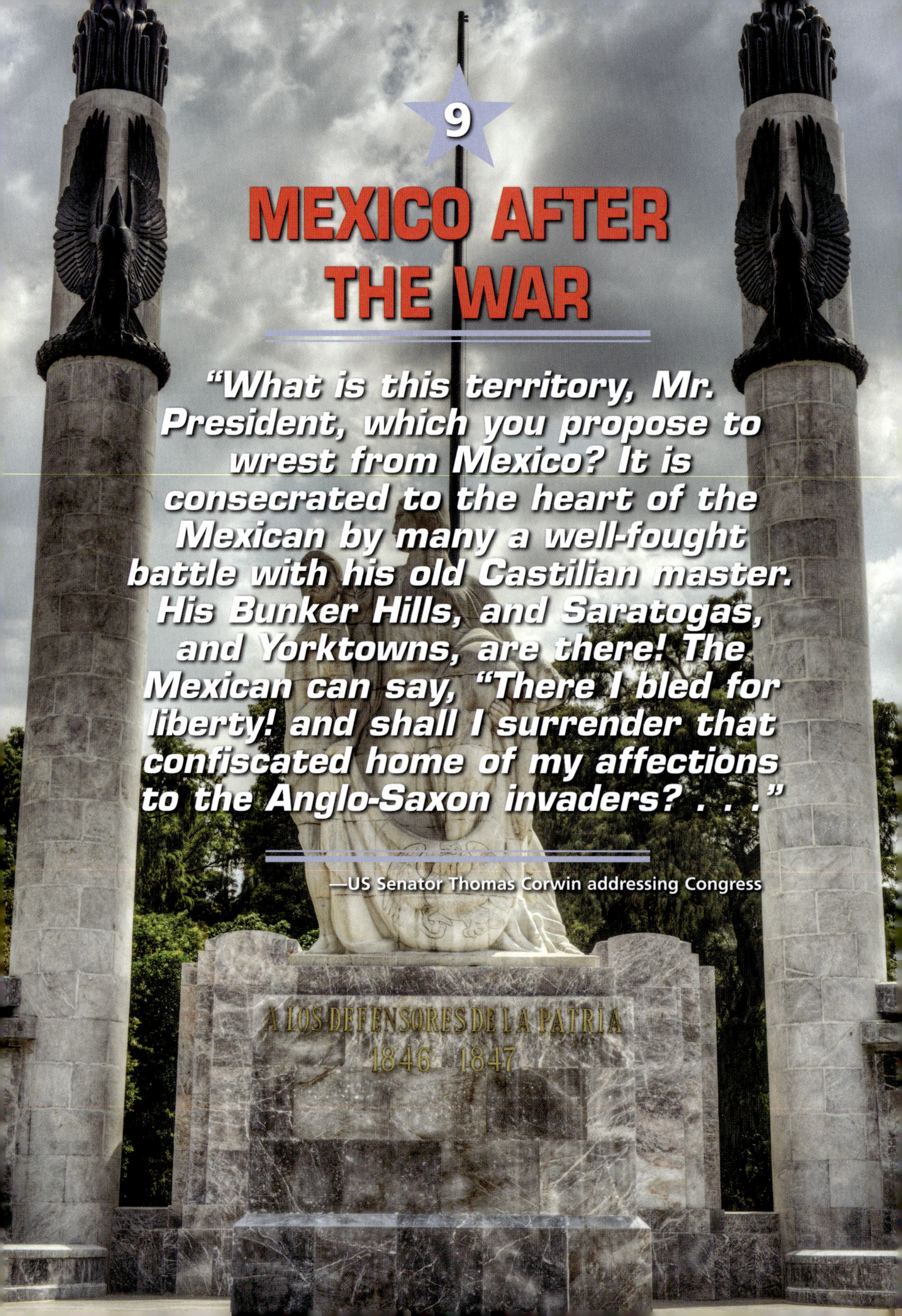

The Mexican-American War was a disaster for Mexico. It forced the nation to surrender about 40 percent of its territory. It also badly weakened the faith of Mexicans in their government, which touched off a major struggle for reform that would go on for over twenty years. The loss of the war also increased the deep mistrust Mexicans had often felt for Americans, and made it strong enough to last for almost one hundred years.

Lost Territory

The Treaty of Guadalupe Hidalgo forced Mexico to give up California and New Mexico to the United States. These vast territories included modern-day California, Nevada, Utah, Arizona, and New Mexico, as well as parts of Colorado and Wyoming. At the time, though, these areas were not well developed economically. Fewer than 100,000 people lived in this huge territory, and most of them made their living by ranching, hunting, trapping, or farming. Americans bought the few products this region had to trade, even in the years before the Mexican-American War. To lose these territories was not a serious blow to the Mexican economy.

However, the loss of California and New Mexico was a serious blow to Mexican pride. The Mexicans had thought of themselves as good fighters ever since 1821, when they had won their war for independence against Spain. Their pride had been hurt a little in 1836 when they lost the Texas War for Independence, but not much, since they had never fully admitted that defeat. Texas was not very big, it had been settled later than the rest of Mexico, and Mexican culture had never really taken root there. Besides, Mexican pride had been restored just two years after losing Texas, when Santa Anna's men threw out the French Army that had captured Veracruz. Losing California and New Mexico, on the other hand, hurt Mexico's national pride a lot. These places had been part of Mexico for 250 years, and Hispanic culture thrived there. These places had made up one third of Mexico's territory. It was a much greater loss than losing Texas, which was only a small percentage of Mexican territory at the time. Imagine how Americans would feel if Canada invaded the United States and captured the states of Minnesota, North and South Dakota, Montana, Idaho, Washington, and Oregon. This is how the Mexicans felt about losing California and New Mexico. Many Mexicans still feel that way today.

The First Mexican Americans

Of course, no Mexicans felt worse about losing these territories than those who lived in them. By moving the border between Mexico and the United States hundreds of miles to the south, the Treaty of Guadalupe Hidalgo created a new ethnic group, Mexican Americans. The treaty offered US citizenship to all Mexicans who lived in the Mexican Cession, and approximately 90 percent accepted the offer. However, most of them continued to think of themselves as Mexicans, not Americans, in terms of language and culture.

Anglos, the term for non-Hispanic whites, thought of them as being Mexican, too. Although they were not supposed to do so, the territorial governments soon passed laws making it difficult for lifelong Mexican residents to serve in the territorial and state governments. Instead, these governments were controlled by newly arrived Americans, who used their influence to obtain—sometimes dishonestly—much of the land that wealthy Mexican ranchers in California and New Mexico had owned.

But not all Mexican-Americans suffered from this sort of discrimination. Some even profited from the transfer of the Mexican Cession to the United States.

Esteban Ochoa is a good example. Born in 1831, Ochoa grew up in Santa Fe. As a teenager, he helped his father with his trading business, which bought and sold goods in the United States and Mexico. After the war, Ochoa started several businesses of his own, including a freight-hauling service, a flour mill, and a string of general stores. By the time he was 30, he was one of the most prosperous businesspeople in New Mexico Territory. He later moved to Arizona Territory where he served as mayor of Tucson and a member of the territorial legislature.[1]

In fact, a number of Mexican-Americans, many of them born in Mexico, held important political offices in the 50 years immediately following the Mexican-American War. For example, the Otero family was prominent in the political affairs of New Mexico Territory between 1850 and 1900. In 1856, Miguel Antonio Otero was elected to represent the territory as a delegate to the US House of Representatives. Twenty years later, his nephew, Mariano Sabino Otero, was elected to the same position. In 1896, his son, Miguel Antonio Otero II, was appointed governor of New Mexico Territory.[2]

Indians on the Warpath

Subduing the various nations of Native Americans that lived in Mexico had been a problem for the Mexicans, and the Spanish before them, ever since the Spanish took control of Mexico. In fact, one reason that the Americans felt justified in taking control of the lands of the Mexican Cession is that the Mexican government had never been able to prevent these nations, such as the Apache,

Miguel Antonio Otero was the first US Representative for New Mexico, when it was still a territory.

Comanche and Navajo, from raiding their farms, ranches, and trade routes. This problem got even worse as a result of the Mexican-American War.

During the war, the Mexican government had to call in its soldiers and militiamen from all across Mexico to try to repel the American invaders. This meant that practically no one was left to keep the Native Americans under control, and many of the groups revolted. After the war was over, the Indians realized that the Americans had almost totally destroyed the Mexican Army. This led to more Indian revolts.

The worst American Indian revolt was the Caste War (1847–1904) in Yucatan. When the Mexican-American War broke out, local authorities in the port city of Campeche raised a battalion of Mayan Indians to help defend against a possible American attack. The attack never came, but in 1847, the battalion revolted against the harsh treatment of Mayan Indians by the Mexican government. The revolt quickly spread across the Yucatan Peninsula, the ancestral homeland of the Mayan people. For six years, the Mayans and Mexicans battled fiercely. At one point the Mayans controlled almost the entire Yucatan Peninsula, and the major cities of Campeche and Merida were filled with non-Indian refugees. The Mayans were temporarily defeated in 1853, but the conflict flared up again in five years later. This time, it took the Mexican government almost fifty years to subdue the Mayans. Even today, there is much ill feeling between Mexicans and Indians on the Yucatan Peninsula.

Native American revolts broke out as a result of the Mexican-American War in other places, too. Between 1848 and 1855, Indians revolted in the states of Oaxaca and Guerrero in the south, Veracruz in the east, Coahuila and Tamaulipas in the northeast, Chihuahua and Durango in the north, and Hidalgo and Tlaxcala in central Mexico. Indian raids were so horrible in the north that large areas were abandoned by non-Indians. Not until the late 1850s was the Mexican military strong enough to restore the government's rule in these places.[3]

New National Heroes

Even though the war gave the Mexicans very little to cheer about, it did give them some new national heroes to celebrate. The most famous ones are Los Niños Héroes, who died at the Battle of Chapultepec.

Los Niños Héroes are remembered in Mexico to this day. In 1947, a large stone monument, pictured in chapter 1, commemorating their sacrifice was erected in the park at the base of Chapultepec Hill. Every year on September 13, the day they died fighting for their country, an impressive ceremony is held in their honor.[4]

Another group that became national heroes in Mexico as a result of the war is the San Patricios, who were also mentioned in Chapter 1. Also known as the Irish Martyrs, the San Patricios were Irish immigrants who had deserted from the US Army and joined the Mexican Army. They fought with great skill and bravery, particularly at the Battle of Churubusco. Thirty of them were hanged for desertion by the Americans after the Battle of Chapultepec. Today, their heroism is remembered on two days. One is September 12, which commemorates the anniversary of their hangings, and the other is March 17, Saint Patrick's Day. Throughout Mexico, a number of streets and schools have been named in their honor. In 1997, Mexican President Ernesto Zedilla commemorated the 150th anniversary of their executions at a ceremony in Mexico City.[5]

Democratic Reform

Many educated Mexicans believed that Mexico lost the war because the country was run poorly. Although Mexico was supposed to be a democracy, most of the real power belonged to the military and the Roman Catholic Church. Every Mexican president from 1821 to 1848 had been a general, so the army got most of the money from tax revenues. In addition to owning thousands of churches and cathedrals, the Church owned a lot of houses and farms. But since the Church was tax-exempt, the government could not collect taxes from any of this property. Mexico also had three different legal systems—one for soldiers, one for priests, and one for everyone else. A soldier or a priest accused of committing a civil crime would be tried in a military or a church court, not in a civil court. This meant that

Mexicans were not equal before the law, which is a basic feature of democracy.

For seven years after the Mexican-American War ended, many educated Mexicans struggled to reform the government. Many of them were sent to jail by the government, which was still controlled by the military. Others had to flee the country. But in 1855, a group of civilian reformers took control of the government and began making changes. They changed the three-court system so that everyone received equal justice. They also tried to make the army and the Church sell any property that was not used for military or religious purposes. In 1857, they approved a new constitution that gave Mexicans most of the basic rights spelled out in the United States Constitution.[6]

The army and the Church, which lost their special privileges, were not happy about these reforms. In 1858, civil war broke out when the army tried to retake control of the government. In response, the reformers raised an army of their own from peasants and middle-class citizens who were tired of the old way of doing things. Known as the War of the Reform, this civil war raged for three years before the reformers won. They were able to win largely because many officers and soldiers left the regular army and joined the reformers' army. However, the civil war exhausted Mexico so much that it could not pay its debts to foreign countries.

In 1861, France once again landed an army in Veracruz with the intention of making Mexico a French colony until Mexican debts to France were repaid. For the next six years, the reformers fought the French until they left the country in 1867. The effort to reform Mexico had taken almost twenty years. No one knows how much it cost in terms of lives and money.[7]

Anti-US Feelings

The Mexican-American War made Mexicans hate Americans. Almost immediately after the war, a number of folk songs were written that expressed fear and hatred of Yankees, as Mexicans called Americans. In later years, when the Mexicans undertook a major railroad construction program, none of them wanted to build a connecting line to the United States because that would give the hated Yankees easier access to Mexico. Ever since the Mexican-American War, many Mexicans have blamed all their country's problems on the United States.[8]

Until 1950, the actions of the United States government did nothing to change this negative attitude. On several occasions, the United States tried to interfere in Mexico's internal affairs. The worst attempt took place between 1910 and 1917, when the United States tried to influence who would be president of Mexico.

In 1911, Francisco Madero, who belonged to one of Mexico's most powerful families, was elected president of Mexico. He seemed hostile to American business interests in Mexico, so the United States secretly gave money and weapons to the rebel forces of Victoriano Huerta, the former Commander in Chief of the Mexican Army. In 1913 Huerta's forces captured and killed Madero, and Huerta became the new president. When he also threatened American business interests, the United States shifted its support to the governor of the state of Coahuila, Venustiano Carranza. In 1914, the Americans seized Veracruz from Huerta's forces, and a few months later Carranza replaced Huerta as president. But when Carranza refused to accept American advice about who should serve in the new Mexican cabinet, the Americans began supporting Pancho Villa, a rebel military leader who had supported Madero but opposed Huerta and Carranza, for president. Unfortunately for Villa, he had little support in Mexico, so the Americans were eventually forced to accept Carranza.

This made Villa angry. In 1916, his small army began killing Americans on both sides of the United States-Mexico border. His men pulled sixteen Americans off a train in northern Mexico and shot them. Then they raided Columbus, New Mexico, and shot seventeen more Americans.

In response, the United States government sent General John J. Pershing, who would later become a hero in World War I, into Mexico with an army to capture Villa and his men. Pershing chased Villa for 300 miles (482 km) into Mexico but never found him. However, Pershing did find a Mexican army that had been sent to stop him. The two armies fought two skirmishes during which forty Mexicans and twelve Americans died. Fortunately, Pershing's army was recalled before another war broke out.[9]

Relations between Mexico and the United States began to improve in 1947 when United States President Harry Truman visited Mexico City. While there, he laid a wreath on the monument to Los

Pancho Villa (center) was one of the most prominent figures of the Mexican Revolution, fought mainly between 1910 – 1920.

Niños Héroes. This symbolic act helped break the ice between the two countries. Not long after Truman's visit, the Congresses of Mexico and the United States voted to return all the flags and other trophies of war that had been captured during the Mexican-American War. Then Mexican President Miguel Aleman visited Washington, and friendly relations between the countries began to develop. Problems such as immigration and trade continue to exist between the two countries, but today, Mexico and the United States seem to be on the road to becoming good neighbors, if not good friends.[10]

Réconquista

A popular theme among Mexicans and Mexican Americans ever since the end of the Mexican-American

War has been the idea of Réconquista, meaning some people think that Mexico should take back the lands lost to the United States during the war. This idea got some serious consideration by the Mexican government in 1917 during World War I. At the time, the United States was at war with Germany, and the Germans offered to help Mexico reclaim Texas and the lands in the Mexican Cession if the Mexicans would declare war against the Americans as German allies. But in the end, the Mexican government turned down the offer because Mexico was not prepared to go to war with the United States again.

Today, a majority of Mexicans believe that the Southwest US rightfully belongs to Mexico. However, Réconquista is talked about mostly in terms of a cultural reclamation instead of a political or military one. Some observers have noted the emergence of Spanglish, a mixture of Spanish and English that is spoken by many throughout the Southwest United States. Speakers of Spanglish will use a Spanish word or phrase to express one idea and then, in the same sentence, use an English word or phrase to express another idea. Other observers have noted the increased popularity over the years of Southwestern cuisine, which uses red and green chili peppers to season food. Today, Mexican restaurants are popular all across the United States, not just in the Southwest. Chipotle Mexican Grill and Chili's Grill and Bar are two chains of casual dining restaurants that have grown rapidly in popularity. One of the most popular fast food restaurants in the US today is

Taco Bell; during the 1990s, their slogan was "Make a Run for the Border."

Although very few people seriously believe that Mexico will regain control of California, Nevada, Utah, Arizona, New Mexico and Texas, the idea remains a hot topic in the popular culture of the Southwest and Mexico.[11]

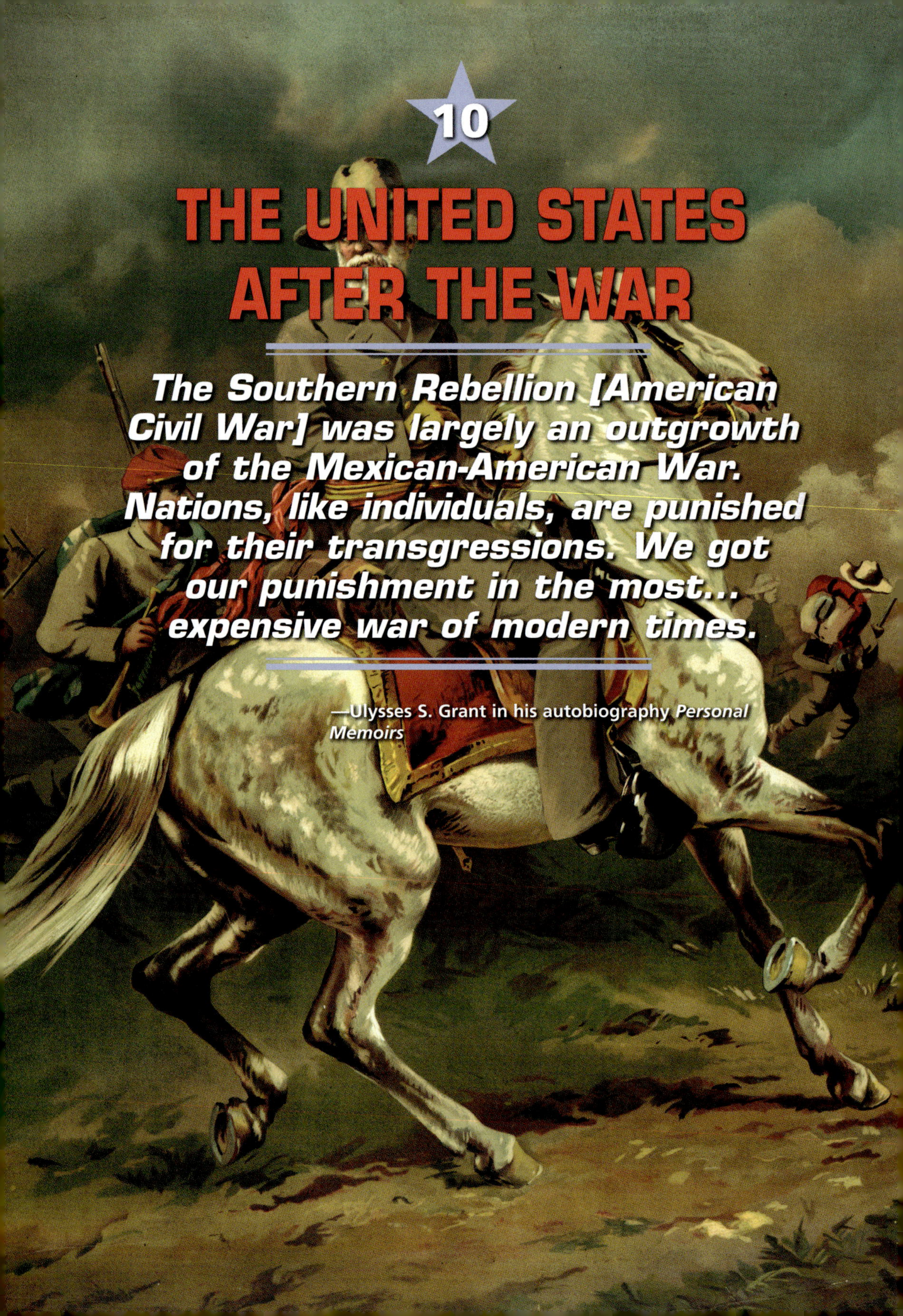

10

THE UNITED STATES AFTER THE WAR

The Southern Rebellion [American Civil War] was largely an outgrowth of the Mexican-American War. Nations, like individuals, are punished for their transgressions. We got our punishment in the most... expensive war of modern times.

—Ulysses S. Grant in his autobiography *Personal Memoirs*

The Mexican-American War also dramatically affected the United States. By winning the war, the United States acquired a huge amount of territory, known as the Mexican Cession.

The Treaty of Guadalupe Hidalgo made the Rio Grande the boundary between the United States and Mexico. It also gave the United States the Mexican territories of California and New Mexico. These territories eventually entered the Union as the states of Arizona, California, Nevada, New Mexico, and Utah.

It would be hard to imagine the United States today without these states. California has more people than any other state in the Union. The important cities of Los Angeles, San Francisco, San Diego, Salt Lake City, Phoenix, Las Vegas, and Santa Fe are all built on land obtained from Mexico in the war. Over the years, this area has supplied the United States with a significant amount of its gold, silver, oil, cattle, fruits, vegetables, and even movies. A number of popular tourist attractions, such as Yosemite and Sequoia National Parks, the Grand Canyon, the Las Vegas casinos, Hollywood, and Disneyland are located in these states.

Pre-Civil War Presidential Politics

The Mexican-American War produced a number of American heroes. Some of them used the popularity they received from the Mexican-American War to run for president. Generals Zachary Taylor and Winfield Scott emerged from the Mexican-American War as national heroes. By leading their armies to victory, both men became very popular all across the United States. This popularity allowed them both to run for president. In 1848, Taylor was elected president on the Whig party ticket, but he died in office after serving only two years. In 1852, the Whigs nominated Winfield Scott for president. He lost to Franklin Pierce, the candidate of the Democrats, who had also served as a general in the Mexican-American War.

Although he did not win the kind of amazing, against-all-odds victories that Taylor and Scott won,

John C. Frémont became famous for his exploits in California during the Mexican-American War. In 1856, the Republican Party made him its first candidate for president. He lost the election, but the Republicans went on to become one of the two major parties in the United States.

At the start of the Civil War, the Confederate States of America, made up of the Southern states that had left the Union, chose Jefferson Davis to be its first and only president. Davis was part of the regiment that helped saved the day at the Battle of Buena Vista.

A Cause of the Civil War

The biggest political issue in the United States during the 1840s and 1850s was slavery. Many Northerners wanted either to abolish slavery or to keep it confined to the Southern states, in order to protect free labor and their political power in Congress. Many were also morally opposed to the practice of slavery. Most Southerners, on the other hand, wanted to expand slavery in order to preserve the way of life they had lived for generations. The issue became an even bigger problem after the Mexican-American War. Neither side could agree whether slavery should be allowed into the new western territories won from Mexico during the war.

The problem of slavery in new territories had been solved through compromise. The 1820 Missouri Compromise drew an imaginary line across the Louisiana Purchase territories at 36°30′ north latitude. Slavery would be permitted south of the line and prohibited north of the line, with the exception of Missouri, because Missouri's southern boundary was the compromise line and slavery had already been established there. Northerners and Southerners were happy with the Missouri Compromise—for a while.

When the United States acquired so much new territory from Mexico, the first question to arise in the nation, which was already being torn by disagreement over slavery, was whether slavery would be permitted there. In fact, the question came up in 1846 even before the war was over. David Wilmot, an antislavery congressman from Pennsylvania, asked Congress to pass a bill prohibiting slavery in any territory the United States might gain during the Mexican-American War. The Wilmot Proviso, as his request was called, was voted down by the Senate, but it began the long debate on the future of slavery in the Mexican Cession.

In addition to the Wilmot Proviso, three other responses to the problem were suggested. Southerners insisted that Congress did not have the power to prohibit people from taking their property or their slaves with them wherever they wanted to go. Therefore, Congress could not keep slaves, who were considered property, out of the Mexican Cession. Other people suggested extending the Missouri Compromise Line, or 36°30', all the way to the Pacific Ocean, permitting slavery south of the line and prohibiting it north of the line. Still others argued that the residents of the Mexican Cession should be allowed to decide for themselves through a vote whether or not to permit slavery. This idea became known as popular sovereignty.

Neither of the two major political parties of the late 1840s, the Democrats and the Whigs, took a stand on the issue of slavery in the Mexican Cession. This angered antislavery members of both parties, who left to form the Free-Soil party. The Free-Soilers' major issue was keeping slavery out of the Mexican Cession. In the election of 1848, they sent ten members to Congress, and their candidate for president polled 10 percent of the popular vote.

The Compromise of 1850 solved the problem for a while by approving popular sovereignty in the new territories of Utah and New Mexico. As part of the same compromise agreement, California was admitted to the Union as a free state.

The real trouble started when the idea of popular sovereignty was applied to territories outside of the Mexican Cession. According to the Missouri Compromise, any states formed from the Kansas and Nebraska territories, which were originally part of the Louisiana Purchase, were supposed to be free from slavery. But Southerners began arguing that, if popular sovereignty could be allowed in Utah and New Mexico, then it should be allowed in Kansas and Nebraska. In 1854, Congress passed the Kansas-Nebraska Act, which set aside the Missouri Compromise so that the voters in Kansas and Nebraska could decide for themselves if theirs would be free or slave states.

Nebraska was so far north that it would probably never be a slave state. But Kansas was no farther north than Missouri, Kentucky, Virginia, and Maryland—all of which were slave states. So there was a real possibility that Kansas might vote to allow slavery. Thousands of proslavery and antislavery settlers rushed to Kansas to influence the vote. Before long, they began shooting at each other.

Many antislavery people were so outraged by the Kansas-Nebraska Act that they formed the Republican Party, which opposed the spread of slavery to the territories. This party was bigger and stronger than the Free-Soil party, since it united people who wanted to prevent the spread of slavery with the abolitionists who wanted to eliminate slavery altogether. In 1860, it succeeded in electing its candidate for the presidency, Abraham Lincoln. When this happened, the South feared that slavery would soon be barred from the territories and eventually from the South as well. In order to protect the future of slavery, eleven Southern states left the Union and the Civil War began.

Many Southerners believed that the Union would let them secede without a war. Most of those who did believe that the United States would fight to keep the southern states in the Union were convinced that the Confederacy would win easily. One reason they believed this was because of the way some northern and southern units fought in the Mexican-American War. Many southerners knew, for example, about the Battle of Buena Vista, and how one southern regiment outfought several northern ones.

Training Generals

Like President Jefferson Davis, a number of Civil War generals also got their first battlefield experience during the Mexican-American War. Many of them played important roles during the Mexican-American War as junior officers.

Robert E. Lee, who eventually became the commanding general of the Confederate Army, was a captain of engineers in Mexico. He provided Zachary Taylor's and Winfield Scott's armies with detailed reports on Mexican defensive positions and scouted out ways to attack them. Ulysses S. Grant, the last commanding general of the Union Army of the Potomac, was an infantry lieutenant in Mexico. He was cited for bravery during the fighting at Molino del Rey. Pierre G. T. Beauregard, commander of the Confederate forces that fired on Fort Sumter to start the Civil War, was a lieutenant of engineers in Mexico. He served primarily as Lee's assistant while the two were assigned to Scott's army. George B. McClellan, first commanding general of the Union Army of the Potomac, was a lieutenant of engineers in Mexico. He was cited for bravery at the battles of Contreras, Churubusco, and Chapultepec.

Braxton Bragg, general of the Confederate Army of Tennessee, and George H. Thomas, general of the Union Army of Tennessee, had been lieutenants of artillery in Mexico. They commanded two of the artillery batteries that stopped the Mexican advance at the Battle of Buena Vista and helped save the day for the Americans. George G. Meade, commanding general of the Union Army of the Potomac at Gettysburg, was a lieutenant of engineers in Mexico. He was cited for bravery during the Battle of Monterrey. James Longstreet, who commanded a corps in Lee's Army of Northern Virginia, was an infantry lieutenant in Scott's army. He is the wounded company commander who handed the regimental flag to George Pickett at the Battle of Chapultepec. During the Civil War, Pickett commanded a division in Longstreet's corps. Thomas J. "Stonewall" Jackson, Lee's top Confederate general during the Civil War until his death in May 1863, was a lieutenant of artillery in Mexico. He was cited for bravery in just about every battle that Scott's army fought.

Robert E. Lee is best known for being the commander of the Confederate Army during the Civil War.

In addition to training lots of generals for both sides in the Civil War, the Mexican-American War also taught those generals two important lessons about how to wage war. The first lesson was how to use a turning movement to get the enemy to abandon their positions. The other lesson was how to extend the supply lines of an invading army by living off the land, a practice known as foraging.

A turning movement is similar to a flanking movement, which is when a small part of an army attempts to attack the enemy from the flank or side while the main part of the army attacks from the front. In a turning movement, the main part of the attacking army attempts to slip around a defenders' flank without being caught while a small part keeps the enemy engaged from the front. This is a tricky maneuver to pull off successfully, but when it works the defending army must abandon its defensive positions without firing a shot so that it doesn't get surrounded and captured. The turning movement had been taught in the classroom for years at the US Military Academy, but until the Mexican-American War American generals had never had a chance to see how well it worked on the battlefield.

The US Army tried to use the turning movement in just about every battle in the Mexican-American War. The best use of the turning movement came when Winfield Scott landed his army at Veracruz and then marched inland to Mexico City. Because Scott was now behind Santa Anna's army, the Mexican general had to withdraw much of his army from its position in front of Zachary Taylor's army in the north and fall back to defend the capital. Scott's successful use of the turning movement helped the United States win the Mexican-American War.

In the early days of the Civil War, Union General George B. McClellan tried to use a turning movement to get around the Confederate army in northern Virginia. Instead of attacking it head-on, McClellan boarded his troops on ships and sailed them up the James River, the same river that Richmond, the Confederate capital, was located on. Sure enough, the Confederates ended up pulling back much of their army in northern Virginia to defend Richmond. Unfortunately for McClellan, the Confederates fought much better against him than the Mexican did against Scott. Even so, McClellan's troops got within a few miles of Richmond and almost captured it. If they had done so, the Civil War might have ended much sooner than it did.[1]

One of the biggest problems in keeping an invading army in the field is keeping it supplied with food, ammunition, and all the other things it needs to fight. The longer an invading army's supply lines stretch, the harder it is to keep supplies flowing smoothly from the army's base to the battlefield. Scott was only about halfway to Mexico City when he realized that his supply lines had been stretched about as thin as they could get. His decision to forage instead of depending on a long supply line meant that his army could keep advancing on the enemy without having to worry about what they were going to eat.

George G. Meade was in charge of the US Army of the Potomac for part of the Civil War.

This same situation occurred during the Civil War after Union General William T. Sherman captured Atlanta, Georgia. Sherman realized that his supply lines, which ran all the way through Tennessee and into Kentucky, could easily be raided by Confederate cavalry. These raids would slow down his army and maybe even keep it from cutting the Confederacy in half by marching to the sea and capturing Savannah, Georgia, on the Atlantic Ocean. So, Sherman decided to do what Scott had done in Mexico. He ordered his men to march through Georgia at a width of about 90 miles (145 km). As they did so, they managed to find enough food to eat so that they could march fast and hard, and before long they had captured Savannah.[2] Without the lessons learned from the Mexican-American War, the Civil War could very well have had a different result.

Indian Wars

The Mexican Cession didn't contain just Mexican farmers and ranchers. It was also home to a number of Native American nations, such as the Apaches, Comanches, and Navajos. Some scholars believe these groups are related to the Aztecs, the fierce warriors who swept down from the North and conquered the Valley of Mexico before the Spanish arrived. In any case, these tribes had resisted fiercely every attempt made by the Spanish and Mexicans to control them, and they had no intention of letting the Americans succeed at this, either. For several decades, these tribes fought almost constantly against the US Army. Their leaders included such famous chiefs as Geronimo and Cochise. Unfortunately for the Indians, they were badly outnumbered, and by 1890 they had been defeated, rounded up and relocated to reservations. But for almost 40 years, they had kept thousands of US troops tied down in the American Southwest.

American Popular Culture

Every ethnic group that has ended up in the United States has helped shape American popular culture, and Mexican Americans are no exception. Today,

Geronimo was a fierce Apache warrior who fought against Mexicans and Americans to keep his people's land and freedom.

their cultural influence is felt in all 50 states, not just the ones that came out of the Mexican-American War. As mentioned before, Mexican-American food, or Southwestern cuisine, is now popular across the country.

One of the more interesting contributions of Mexican-American culture to US popular culture is the holiday known as Cinco de Mayo. This holiday celebrates the victory, on May 5, 1862, of the Mexican Army over an invasion force of French troops that was larger and better equipped. Although the holiday is hardly celebrated at all in Mexico, it became very popular in California and spread from there throughout the Mexican-American community. In the 1980s, American beer companies began promoting Cinco de Mayo as an excuse to celebrate (by using their products, of course). Today, Cinco de Mayo has taken its place among the most popular ethnic holidays such as St. Patrick's Day and Columbus Day.

The End of Manifest Destiny

The Mexican-American War put an end to Manifest Destiny for a while. Although Americans still wanted their country to expand and grow, the sectional crisis that the Mexican-American War helped create took up the nation's attention for many years. In the

1890s, however, Manifest Destiny reappeared. This time, it was partly responsible for getting the United States involved in the Spanish-American War of 1898, during which the United States acquired Puerto Rico and the Philippines from Spain. But after fighting a long and bloody war with the Filipinos who wanted to be independent, Americans backed away from acquiring any more foreign territory.

Americans had mixed feelings about the Mexican-American War after it ended. Many thought the war was unjustifiable, and said that the United States had deliberately picked a fight with its weaker neighbor. However, the war also helped the United States expand to the size it is today and paved the way for the United States to become a dominant world power.

Chronology

1803—Louisiana Purchase made.

1819—Adams-Onis Treaty cedes Florida to the US and establishes the boundary between the US and New Spain.

1821—Mexico wins its independence from Spain.

1836—Spain recognizes Mexico's independence; Texas declares its independence from Mexico; Battles of the Alamo, Goliad, and San Jacinto take place; Texas applies for admission to the United States.

1842—US Navy occupies Monterey, California; Santa Anna returns from exile, becoming dictator of Mexico.

1844 —James Polk elected president of the United States.

1845—United States tries to buy California and New Mexico from Mexico; Texas admitted to the United States.

March 1846—US Army occupies Texas south of the Nueces River.

April 1846—Fighting breaks out between United States and Mexico.

May 8–9, 1846—Battles of Palo Alto and Resaca de la Palma take place.

May 13, 1846—United States declares war on Mexico.

June 1846—Bear Flag Republic declared in California.

August 1846—American forces occupy Santa Fe, New Mexico.

September 20–24, 1846—Battle of Monterrey.

December 6, 1846—Battle of San Pasqual.

January 8, 1847—Battle of San Gabriel.

January 13, 1847—United States takes control of California.

February 22–23, 1847—Battle of Buena Vista.

February 28, 1847—Battle of Río Sacramento.

March 29, 1847— Americans capture Veracruz.

April 17–18, 1847—Battle of Cerro Gordo.

May 15–29, 1847—Americans enter Puebla.

August 19–20, 1847—Battles of Padierna/Contreras and Churubusco take place.

September 12–13, 1847—Battle of Chapultepec.

September 14, 1847—US Army enters Mexico City.

February 2, 1848—Treaty of Guadalupe Hidalgo signed.

March10, 1848—US Congress ratifies Treaty of Guadalupe Hidalgo.

May 25, 1848—Mexican Congress ratifies Treaty of Guadalupe Hidalgo.

Chapter Notes

FOREWORD

1 Collier, Christopher, and James Lincoln Collier, *Hispanic America, Texas, and the Mexican-American War: 1835-1850* (Marshall Cavendish Corp., 1998), p. 89.

CHAPTER 1. HEROES AND HANGINGS

1 Edward G. Longacre, *Pickett, Leader of the Charge: A Biography of General George E. Pickett, C.S.A.* (White Mane Publishing Co.), 1995, p. 26.

2. Mark Crawford, ed., *Encyclopedia of the Mexican-American War* (Santa Barbara, Calif.: ABC-CLIO, 1999), p. 201.

3. Edward H. Moseley and Paul C. Clark, Jr., *Historical Dictionary of the United States-Mexican-American War* (Lanham, Md.: Scarecrow Press, 1997), pp. 244–245.

CHAPTER 2. WHY WAS THE MEXICAN-AMERICAN WAR FOUGHT?

1. Humanities Texas, *Invasion Yanqui: The Mexican-American War, 1846–1848*, 2015, http://www.humanitiestexas.org/news/events/invasión-yanqui-us-mexican-war-1846-1848.
2. John M. Murrin et al., *Liberty, Equality, Power: A History of the American People* (Fort Worth, Tex.: Harcourt Brace College Publishers, 1999), pp. 296–298.
3. Robert W. Merry, *A Country of Vast Designs: James K. Polk, the Mexican-American War, and the Conquest of the American Continent* (New York: Simon and Schuster, 2009), pp. 9, 10, 70.
4. Murrin, pp. 435–438.
5. Hampton Sides, *Blood and Thunder: The Epic Story of Kit Carson and the Conquest of the American West*. (New York: Anchor Books, 2006), pp. 56–59.
6. Murrin, p. 442–44.

7. Merry, pp. 70–71.
8. John S. D. Eisenhower, *So Far From God: The U.S. War with Mexico, 1846–1848* (New York: Random House, 1989), pp. 13–14.
9.Murrin, p. 444.
10. Merry, 194, 209–211.
11. Merry, pp. 188, 219, 241–242.
12. Murrin, pp. 444–445.

CHAPTER 3. ZACHARY TAYLOR AND THE ARMY OF THE NORTH

1. K. Jack Bauer, *Zachary Taylor: Soldier, Planter, Statesman of the Old Southwest* (Baton Rouge: Louisiana State University Press, 1985), p. 94.
2. John S. D. Eisenhower, *So Far From God: The U.S. War with Mexico, 1846–1848* (New York: Random House, 1989), pp. 54–65.
3. Cecil Robinson, ed., *The View From Chapultepec: Mexican Writers on the Mexican-American War* (Tucson: University of Arizona Press, 1989), p. 46.
4. Richard B. Winders, *Mr. Polk's Army: The American Military Experience in the Mexican-American War* (College Station: Texas A & M University Press, 2000), p. 90.
5. Ibid., pp. 71–73.
6. Eisenhower, pp. 73–74.
7. Robert W. Merry, *A Country of Vast Designs: James K. Polk, the Mexican-American War, and the Conquest of the American Continent*. New York: Simon and Schuster, 2009, p. 259.
8. Ibid., pp. 83–85.
9. Merry, pp. 259-60.
10. Eisenhower pp. 100–112.
11. Ibid., pp. 113, 120.
12. Merry, pp. 310–311.
13. T. Harry Williams, *The History of American Wars From 1745 to 1918* (New York: Alfred A. Knopf, 1981), p. 172.

14. John S. D. Eisenhower, *So Far From God: The U.S. War With Mexico, 1846–1848* (New York: Random House, 1989), pp. 132–133.
15. Ibid., pp. 135–137.
16. Ibid., p. 138.
17. Ibid., p. 140.
18. Merry, p. 312.
19. Eisenhower, pp. 143, 149.

CHAPTER 4. THE RETURN OF SANTA ANNA

1. Ruth R. Olivera and Liliance Crete, *Life in Mexico Under Santa Anna, 1822–1855* (Norman: University of Oklahoma Press, 1991), pp. 29–30.
2. Eisenhower, p. 187.
3. Robert W. Merry, *A Country of Vast Designs: James K. Polk, the Mexican-American War, and the Conquest of the American Continent*. (New York: Simon and Schuster, 2009), pp. 353–354.

CHAPTER 5. STEPHEN KEARNY AND THE ARMY OF THE WEST

1. John M. Murrin et al., *Liberty, Equality, Power: A History of the American People* (Forth Worth, Tex.: Harcourt Brace College Publishers, 1999), pp. 437–438.
2. Hampton Sides, *Blood and Thunder: The Epic Story of Kit Carson and the Conquest of the American West*. (New York: Anchor Books, 2006), pp. 346-348.
3. Sides, pp. 29-32, 67-74.
4. Sides, pp. 101–106, 111–115, 127–134.
5. Murrin, p. 438.
6. John S. D. Eisenhower, *So Far From God: The U.S. War with Mexico, 1846–1848* (New York: Random House, 1989), pp. 200–203.
7. Sides, pp. 86–89.
8. Sides, pp. 117–120.
9. Sides, pp. 121–126, 176–177.

10. Sides, pp. 185–205.
11. Eisenhower, pp. 226–229.

CHAPTER 6. WINFIELD SCOTT AND THE ARMY OF THE EAST

1. Timothy D. Johnson, *Winfield Scott: The Quest for Military Glory* (Lawrence: University Press of Kansas, 1998), p. 227.
2. Ibid., pp. 2, 153.
3. Mark Crawford, ed., *Encyclopedia of the Mexican-American War* (Santa Barbara, Calif.: ABC-CLIO, 1999), p. 261.
4. Amy S. Greenberg, *A Wicked War: Polk, Clay, Lincoln, and the 1848 U.S. Invasion of Mexico* (New York: Alfred A. Knopf, 2012), pp. 168–171.
5. Crawford, p. 20.
6. Eisenhower, pp. 278–279.
7. Ibid., pp. 279–283, 295.,
8. Crawford, pp. 71–73.
9. Eisenhower, pp. 269, 296.

CHAPTER 7. FIGHTING FOR MEXICO CITY

1. John S. D. Eisenhower, *So Far From God: The U.S. War with Mexico, 1846–1848* (New York: Random House, 1989), pp. 298, 302, 306.
2. Amy S. Greenberg, *A Wicked War: Polk, Clay, Lincoln, and the 1848 U.S. Invasion of Mexico*. New York: Alfred A. Knopf, 2012, pp. 207–208.
3. Ibid. , p. 208.
4. Eisenhower, pp. 319–321.
5. Edward H. Moseley and Paul C. Clark, Jr., *Historical Dictionary of the United States–Mexican-American War* (Lanham, Md.: Scarecrow Press, 1997), p. 88.
6. Eisenhower, p. 325.
7. Ibid., p. 327.
8. Greenberg, p. 209.
9. Ibid., pp. 332–338.

10. Ibid., pp. 337–339.
11. Ibid., pp. 338–342.

CHAPTER 8. THE TREATY OF GUADALUPE HIDALGO

1. Robert W. Merry, *A Country of Vast Designs: James K. Polk, the Mexican-American War, and the Conquest of the American Continent*. (New York: Simon and Schuster, 2009), pp. 359–360.
2. John S. D. Eisenhower, *So Far From God: The U.S. War With Mexico, 1846–1848* (New York: Random House, 1989), pp. 305–307.
3. Eisenhower, pp. 360–361.
4. Merry, pp. 424–426.
5. Amy S. Greenberg, *A Wicked War: Polk, Clay, Lincoln, and the 1848 U.S. Invasion of Mexico*. (New York: Alfred A. Knopf, 2012), p. 259.
6. Eisenhower, pp. 366–367.
7. Merry, pp. 433, 448.

CHAPTER 9. MEXICO AFTER THE WAR

1. Matt S. Meier, "Esteban Ochoa, Enterpriser," *Journal of the West* 25, no. 1 (January 1986), pp. 15–21.
2. Otero, Miguel Antonio II. *My Life on the Frontier, 1864-1882.* (New York, 1935.)
3. Ruth R. Olivera and Liliance Crete, *Life in Mexico Under Santa Anna, 1822–1855* (Norman: University of Oklahoma Press, 1991), p. 174; Edward H. Moseley and Paul C. Clark, Jr., *Historical Dictionary of the United States–Mexican-American War* (Lanham, Md.: Scarecrow Press, 1997), pp. 71–72.
4. Michael C. Meyer, *The Course of Mexican History* (New York: Oxford University Press, 1979), p. 352; Howard F. Cline, *The United States and Mexico* (Cambridge, Mass.: Harvard University Press, 1965), p. 313.
5. Martin Paredes, *Batallon de San Patricio: The Irish Heroes of Mexico,* March 2008, www.stpatricksbattalion.org.
6. Meyer, pp. 373–380.

7. Ibid., pp. 381–401.
8. Charles C. Cumberland, *Mexico: The Struggle for Modernity* (New York: Oxford University Press, 1968), p. 211.
9. John M. Murrin et al., *Liberty, Equality, Power: A History of the American People*, 2nd ed. (Fort Worth, Tex.: Harcourt Brace College, 1999), pp. 758–759.
10. Howard F. Cline, *The United States and Mexico* (Cambridge: Harvard University Press), 1953, pp. 313–314.
11. John Bennett, "Amnesty and Historical Guilt: the Mexican-American War," *American Thinker,* June 2, 2013, http://americanthinker.com/articles/2013/06/amnesty_and_historical_guilt_the_mexican_american_war.html.

CHAPTER 10. THE UNITED STATES AFTER THE WAR

1. Herman Hattaway and Archer Jones, *How the North Won: A Military History of the Civil War* (Urbana: University of Illinois Press), 1983, pp. 14–17.
2. Ibid., p. 634.

Glossary

annexation—The action of joining something to something else, often a territory.

artillery—Large guns used in warfare.

Aztecs—A tribe of Indians that conquered the Toltecs and took control of Mexico in the early 1400s

battalion—A large body of troops ready for battle.

batteries—An artillery subunit of guns, men, and vehicles.

casualties—Deaths during a war.

dragoons—A mounted unit; another term for a cavalry unit.

Gila River—a river in Arizona that marked part of the boundary between the United States and Mexico

guerillas—A small independent group of fighters, using irregular tactics, often fighting agains a larger regular force.

infantry—Foot soldiers.

Los Niños Heroes— Eight young military cadets who died fighting for Mexico during the Mexican War

Louisiana Purchase— The purchase by the United States of lands west of the Mississippi River that brought the United States in close contact with the Spanish colony that later became Mexico

Manifest Destiny— The idea that the United States should govern all the lands between the Atlantic and Pacific Oceans

Mexican Cession— The lands surrendered to the United States by Mexico after the conclusion of the Mexican War

Monroe Doctrine— President James Monroe's declaration that the United States would not tolerate European interference in North and South America

Nueces River— A river in Texas that the Mexicans claimed formed part of the northern boundary of Mexico

reconquista— The idea that Mexico should retake the lands lost to the United States as a result of the Mexican War

Rio Grande River— A river in Texas that forms part the boundary between Mexico and the United States

Toltecs— The Indian tribe that ruled Mexico before the Aztec invasion

Treaty of Guadalupe-Hidalgo— The peace treaty that formally ended the Mexican War

For More Information

Books

Cantor, Carrie Michols. *The Mexican-American War: How the United States Gained Its Western Lands*. North Mankato, MN: Child's World, 2013.

DiConsiglio, John. *The Mexican-American War*. Portsmouth, NH: Heinemann Library, 2012.

Porterfield, Jason. *The Treaty of Guadalupe-Hidalgo, 1848: A Primary Source Examination of the Treaty that Ended the Mexican-American War*. New York: Rosen Pub., 2006.

Poulakidas, Georgene. *The Mexican-American War*. New York: Rosen Pub., 2006.

Stein, R. Conrad. *The Mexican-American War*. Greensboro, NC: Morgan Reynolds, 2012.

Websites

A Guide to the Mexican-American War, Library of Congress
www.loc.gov/rr/program/bib/mexicanwar/
A collection or primary documents and images related to the Mexican-American War.

Lincoln/Net: The Mexican-American War, Northern Illinois University
lincoln-live.lib.niu.edu/mexicanamerican
A historical overwiew of the war, and primary documents and images related to it.

Videos

History Channel
www.history.com/topics/mexican-american-war/videos
A series of short videos related to the Meixican-American War and some of its key players.

"The Mexican-American War. "
A&E Home Video. 2008.
A documentary about the Mexican-American War.

Index